MANAGING YOUR SUBCONSCIOUS MIND AND EMOTIONS

Techniques To Resist
Negativity, Stay Focused
And Positive, And Find
Happiness In Daily Activities.

NICCI BROCHARD
&
DR. BEN CHUBA

MANAGING YOUR SUBCONSCIOUS MIND AND EMOTIONS

Techniques To Resist
Negativity, Stay Focused
And Positive, And Find
Happiness In Daily Activities.

CROSSBORDER

New York, London, Quebec

Also published by Nicci Brochard and Dr. Ben Chuba

CONTENTS

FORWARD

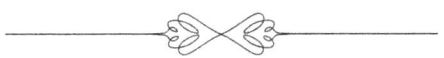

The Power Within

Have you ever felt like your mind was working against you pulling you into negativity, distracting you from your goals, or making happiness seem just out of reach? You are not alone. The human mind is both our greatest ally and our toughest opponent. It can either propel us toward success and fulfillment or trap us in a cycle of doubt, fear, and frustration. But what if you could train your mind to work for you instead of against you?

The truth is, the quality of your life is determined not by your circumstances, but by how you perceive and respond to them. Imagine waking up each day with a deep sense of peace, no matter what challenges await. Imagine being able to resist negativity whether it comes from others or your own inner dialogue. Imagine staying focused and positive, even when life feels chaotic. These abilities are not reserved for the enlightened few; they are skills that anyone can develop.

This book is your guide to harnessing the power of your mind and emotions. You will learn practical techniques to silence self-doubt, break free from negative thought patterns, and cultivate a mindset of resilience and joy. Through simple yet transformative practices, you will discover how to shift your perspective, find meaning in everyday moments, and create a life that feels truly fulfilling.

Your mind is an incredible tool, and when used correctly, it can unlock limitless possibilities. The path to a more focused, positive, and happy life starts now. Are you ready to take control?

Come with us.

THE MIND-EMOTION CONNECTION

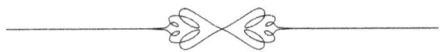

The Power of a Single Thought

Imagine you wake up to a notification on your phone: an email from your boss. The subject line is vague: "Meeting at 10 AM." Instantly, your heart beats faster. Your mind races through scenarios: *Am I in trouble? Did I forget something important?* Anxiety sets in before you even open the email.

Later, when you finally read the message, you realize it's just a routine check-in. The panic was unnecessary. But why did your mind react so strongly? What caused the spiral of emotion that followed a simple email notification?

This scenario illustrates the intricate link between thoughts and emotions. A single thought *this meeting might be bad news,* sparked a cascade of physical and emotional reactions. This mind-emotion connection influences our decisions, interactions, and well-being daily. But how does it work? And, more importantly, how can we harness it to create a more balanced, fulfilling life?

The Science of Thought and Emotion

Thoughts and emotions are not separate entities; they exist in an interconnected feedback loop. Cognitive science and psychology have extensively studied this relationship, uncovering fascinating insights into how our brains process emotions based on our mental narratives.

At the core of this connection is the limbic system, particularly the amygdala, which processes emotions such as fear and pleasure. When a thought arises, like anticipating lousy news, the amygdala reacts instantly, signaling stress responses. Meanwhile, the prefrontal cortex, responsible for reasoning, attempts to evaluate the situation logically. However, if emotions are overwhelming, rational thought takes a backseat, leading to reactive rather than intentional behaviors.

This explains why self-doubt, anxiety, or even joy can arise from internal dialogues rather than external reality. Our emotions are often less about what is happening and more about how we interpret what is happening.

Neuroplasticity: Rewiring Emotional Responses

Neuroscience has shattered the old belief that the brain is static. Neuroplasticity, the brain's ability to rewire itself, allows us to change long-standing emotional patterns and responses. This means that how we react to stress, criticism, or challenges is not fixed; it can be reshaped through intentional practice.

Consider someone who has struggled with self-worth due to years of internalized criticism. Each time they face a challenge, their immediate thought is, *I'm not good enough.* This thought triggers emotions like insecurity and anxiety. However, by deliberately replacing this thought with a new one *I am learning and improving*, they can gradually weaken the old neural pathway and strengthen a healthier, more empowering one.

Studies show that mindfulness practices, cognitive restructuring, and positive reinforcement can create these changes at a neural level. The brain learns from repetition, meaning consciously choosing new thoughts repeatedly will eventually make them automatic.

The Shadow of the Past: How Experiences Shape Mental Patterns

Our present emotions are often influenced by past experiences. From childhood, our minds absorb patterns of how to react to stress, what love looks like, whether we are "enough." These patterns shape our current thought processes, often without us realizing it.

For example, someone who grew up in a critical environment may develop a tendency to self-criticize even when there is no external judgment. Their past has wired their brain to expect negativity, leading them to perceive neutral or even positive situations through a negative lens.

Recognizing these ingrained patterns is crucial in breaking free from them. Self-awareness allows us to pause and question whether our reactions stem from the present reality or from old, unchallenged beliefs.

The Role of Self-Awareness in Transforming Mindsets

Self-awareness is the first step to mastering the mind-emotion connection. It allows us to observe our thoughts without immediately reacting to them. Instead of getting lost in an emotional storm, we can step back and ask:

- Is this thought based on facts or assumptions?
- What emotion is this thought triggering?
- Have I felt this way before in similar situations?
- Can I choose a different perspective?

This reflective approach is often called metacognition, thinking about our thinking. By developing metacognitive awareness, we can break habitual emotional reactions and replace them with intentional, constructive responses.

Identifying Emotional Triggers: A Practical Approach

Emotional triggers are external events or internal thoughts that provoke strong emotional responses. Some common triggers include:

- **Criticism** → Triggers feelings of inadequacy or rejection
- **Failure** → Evokes shame or self-doubt
- **Being ignored** → Sparks feelings of unworthiness
- **Lack of control** → Leads to anxiety or frustration

Identifying triggers requires observation. Keeping an emotional journal can help track patterns by noting what happened, what thoughts arose, and what emotions followed. Over time, this awareness enables us to predict and manage emotional reactions before they take over.

Practical Exercises to Strengthen the Mind-Emotion Connection

1. The Thought-Emotion Journal

Each day, write down:

- A situation that triggered a strong emotion
- The thought that arose from it
- The emotion that followed

- A possible alternative thought that could have led to a different emotional outcome

This practice rewires the brain to seek balanced perspectives rather than reactive patterns.

2. The 10-Second Rule

Before reacting to an emotionally charged situation, pause for ten seconds. Take a deep breath, acknowledge your emotion, and ask: *Is my response based on reality or perception?*

This moment of reflection can prevent impulsive reactions and create space for more mindful decisions.

3. Reframing Negative Thoughts

When you catch yourself in a negative thought spiral, practice reframing by asking:

- What is another way to look at this?
- What would I say to a friend in this situation?
- How does this thought serve me?

By shifting perspectives, we reduce the emotional grip of negative thinking.

4. Mindful Body Scanning

Since emotions manifest physically, a quick body scan can provide insight into how emotions affect you. Take five minutes to notice tension in your body and consciously relax those areas. This practice bridges the gap between mind and body awareness.

5. Gratitude Shift

When overwhelmed by negative emotions, list three things you are grateful for. This simple exercise refocuses the mind on positive realities, reducing the intensity of distressing emotions.

Conclusion: Mastering the Mind-Emotion Connection

The relationship between thoughts and emotions is at the heart of human experience. Understanding it allows us to reclaim control over how we feel and respond to life's challenges.

By leveraging neuroplasticity, becoming self-aware, and practicing intentional thought shifts, we can transform our mental and emotional patterns. Instead of being at the mercy of unconscious reactions, we can become architects of our inner world.

This journey doesn't happen overnight. But with consistent effort, emotional intelligence grows, mental clarity strengthens, and life becomes a space of greater calm, resilience, and fulfillment.

CHAPTER 2

BREAKING FREE FROM NEGATIVITY

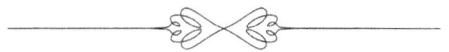

*D*id you know that the average person has about 60,000 thoughts per day, and nearly 80% of them are negative? This staggering statistic sheds light on how much our minds tend to gravitate toward pessimism. But why? Our brains are wired to focus on threats, a survival mechanism inherited from our ancestors. While this instinct was useful in protecting early humans from predators, in today's world, it often leads us into cycles of worry, self-doubt, and anxiety. Fortunately, we don't have to remain prisoners of our own minds. By understanding how negativity manifests and implementing effective strategies, we can break free from its grip and cultivate a more optimistic and resilient mindset.

Recognizing Negative Thought Patterns and Their Impact

Negativity often creeps into our thoughts so subtly that we hardly recognize it. It manifests as self-criticism, doubt, or the constant expectation that things will go wrong. These thought patterns influence how we perceive ourselves and the world around us. When left unchecked, they can lead to anxiety, depression, and even physical health problems such as high blood pressure and weakened immune function.

Negative thinking also affects our relationships, productivity, and overall well-being. Imagine waking up and telling yourself, "Today is going to be awful." Your mind immediately starts looking for evidence to confirm this belief. A spilled coffee, a traffic jam, or a simple misunderstanding with a colleague suddenly reinforce your assumption, perpetuating a self-fulfilling prophecy. By becoming aware of these patterns, you can begin to challenge them before they take hold.

Common Cognitive Distortions and How to Counteract Them

Cognitive distortions are irrational ways of thinking that skew our perception of reality. Here are some of the most common ones, along with strategies to counteract them:

1. **All-or-Nothing Thinking** – Viewing situations in extremes, such as seeing things as entirely good or bad with no middle ground. *Counteract it:* Recognize that life exists in shades of gray. Instead of thinking, "I completely failed that presentation," reframe it as, "I made some mistakes, but I also had strong points."

2. **Overgeneralization** – Making broad conclusions based on a single event. *Counteract it:* If you fail at one task, resist the urge to say, "I always mess things up." Instead, acknowledge it as a single event and move forward.

3. **Catastrophizing** – Assuming the worst-case scenario will happen. *Counteract it:* Ask yourself, "What is the most likely outcome?" More often than not, it's far less disastrous than your mind suggests.

4. **Mind Reading** – Assuming you know what others are thinking, often in a negative way. *Counteract it:* Remind

yourself that you cannot read minds. If you're unsure how someone feels, ask rather than assume.

5. **Should Statements** – Holding yourself to unrealistic standards and feeling guilty when you don't meet them. *Counteract it:* Replace "should" with "could." Instead of saying, "I should be more successful by now," say, "I could take steps to improve my situation."

By recognizing and challenging these distortions, you gain greater control over your thoughts and emotions.

Reframing Challenges as Opportunities for Growth

One of the most powerful ways to break free from negativity is to shift your mindset regarding challenges. Instead of viewing obstacles as insurmountable problems, see them as opportunities for learning and personal growth.

Consider Thomas Edison's perspective when inventing the lightbulb. After thousands of failed attempts, he didn't see himself as a failure. Instead, he famously said, "I have not failed. I've just found 10,000 ways that won't work." This mindset shift is the key to resilience.

To cultivate this perspective in your own life, try the following steps:

- **Identify lessons in setbacks.** Ask yourself, "What can I learn from this experience?"
- **Reframe negative events with empowering language.** Instead of saying, "I can't handle this," try, "This is tough, but I'm capable of figuring it out."
- **Celebrate small wins.** Recognizing progress, no matter how minor, builds confidence and motivation.

By reframing difficulties, you train your brain to focus on solutions rather than problems.

Strategies for Cultivating Optimism in Difficult Situations

Optimism is not about ignoring reality or pretending everything is perfect. It's about choosing to focus on what can go right rather than what can go wrong. Developing optimism in challenging situations requires intentional practice. Here are some strategies to help:

1. **Gratitude Practice** – Regularly reflecting on what you're grateful for helps shift your focus from what's lacking to what's abundant in your life.

2. **Surround Yourself with Positivity** – Engage with people who uplift and inspire you, as negativity can be contagious.

3. **Limit Exposure to Negative Influences** – Reduce time spent on distressing news or social media that fosters comparison and self-doubt.

4. **Engage in Activities That Boost Your Mood** – Exercise, hobbies, and creative pursuits increase dopamine levels and improve mental health.

5. **Adopt a Solution-Oriented Mindset** – When faced with a problem, focus on what actions you can take instead of dwelling on what's wrong.

These small, consistent habits can lead to a lasting shift in perspective.

How to Stop Dwelling on the Past and Worrying About the Future

A significant source of negativity stems from either dwelling on past regrets or worrying excessively about the future. The mind constantly replays old mistakes or anticipates worst-case scenarios, stealing joy from the present moment.

To break free from this cycle:

- **Practice Mindfulness:** Ground yourself in the present through techniques like deep breathing, meditation, or simply focusing on the sensations around you.

- **Challenge Regretful Thoughts:** Remind yourself that the past cannot be changed, but your present actions can shape a better future.

- **Limit "What If" Thinking:** When you catch yourself worrying about things beyond your control, shift your focus to what you can influence.

- **Create a "Let It Go" Ritual:** Write down past regrets or worries on paper and symbolically discard them, reinforcing your decision to move forward.

Living in the present frees up mental space for creativity, joy, and fulfillment.

Conclusion

Breaking free from negativity is not about eliminating difficult emotions altogether. it's about managing them in a way that promotes growth and well-being. By recognizing negative thought patterns, challenging cognitive distortions, reframing challenges, cultivating optimism, and staying present, you can transform your mindset and improve your overall quality of life.

Remember, your thoughts shape your reality. By choosing to focus on the positive, you empower yourself to lead a more fulfilling and resilient life.

THE ART OF EMOTIONAL RESILIENCE

D id you know that astronauts undergo rigorous psychological training before embarking on space missions, not just to withstand physical stress but to maintain emotional resilience in the face of extreme isolation and unpredictability? This highlights a profound truth resilience is not merely about surviving challenges but thriving amidst them. Emotional resilience is an art, a skill that, when honed, can transform life's most difficult moments into opportunities for growth and renewal.

Understanding Emotional Resilience

Emotional resilience refers to the ability to adapt, recover, and even grow in the face of adversity. It's not about avoiding negative emotions but rather about navigating through them with awareness and strength. People with high emotional resilience experience stress, failure, and setbacks just like anyone else, but they have developed the capacity to manage their responses constructively. Resilience is not an inherent trait but a learned skill, shaped by experiences, mindset, and daily habits.

At its core, emotional resilience allows individuals to maintain their equilibrium despite facing personal or professional crises. It involves a mix of self-awareness, cognitive flexibility, emotional regulation, and social support. While some individuals may have a natural inclination toward resilience due to genetic or environmental factors, anyone can cultivate this trait through intentional effort and practice.

Techniques to Stay Composed Under Pressure

Stressful situations are an inevitable part of life. Whether it's a tight deadline, a difficult conversation, or an unexpected loss, how one responds to pressure determines their level of emotional resilience. Below are effective techniques to maintain composure in the face of adversity:

1. **Breathwork and Grounding Exercises** One of the simplest yet most effective ways to regain composure is through controlled breathing techniques. Methods such as box breathing (inhaling for four seconds, holding for four seconds, exhaling for four seconds, and holding again) help regulate the nervous system. Grounding exercises, like focusing on physical sensations (the feel of the ground beneath your feet or the temperature of your surroundings), can anchor you in the present moment and prevent emotional overwhelm.

2. **Cognitive Reframing** The way we interpret situations directly affects our emotional response. Cognitive reframing involves shifting perspective to view challenges as opportunities for growth rather than insurmountable obstacles. Instead of seeing failure as an endpoint, resilient individuals recognize it as part of the learning process.

3. **Mental Rehearsal** Preparing for high-pressure situations by mentally rehearsing different outcomes can enhance resilience. Visualization techniques help create a sense of preparedness, reducing the fear of uncertainty and

boosting confidence in one's ability to handle stress effectively.

4. **Leveraging Support Systems** Humans are wired for connection. Seeking support from trusted friends, mentors, or therapists during challenging times provides a fresh perspective and emotional reinforcement. Resilient individuals know when to ask for help and do not view it as a sign of weakness.

5. **Practicing Emotional Agility** Coined by psychologist Susan David, emotional agility refers to the ability to navigate emotions with flexibility rather than rigidity. Acknowledging and accepting emotions without judgment allows for a more balanced and constructive response to stress.

Developing a Mindset That Embraces Change and Uncertainty

Change is the only constant in life, yet many people resist it, fearing the unknown. Developing a mindset that embraces uncertainty is a cornerstone of emotional resilience. Here's how to cultivate it:

1. **Adopt a Growth Mindset** Individuals with a growth mindset, as defined by psychologist Carol Dweck, view challenges as opportunities to develop their abilities. Rather than fearing failure, they see it as a steppingstone to mastery.

2. **Find Stability Within** External circumstances may be unpredictable, but internal stability can be cultivated. Practices such as mindfulness, journaling, and meditation create a strong inner foundation that remains steady despite external chaos.

3. **Detach from the Illusion of Control** Resilient individuals focus on what they can control and let go of what they cannot. Learning to surrender to uncertainty while remaining adaptable fosters a sense of peace and readiness for change.

4. **Reframe Uncertainty as Excitement** The physiological response to fear and excitement is similar; both involve heightened alertness and an increased heart rate. Reframing uncertainty as a source of excitement rather than dread shifts the mindset from resistance to anticipation.

The Importance of Self-Compassion in Tough Times

Self-compassion is often overlooked but is a crucial component of emotional resilience. It involves treating oneself with kindness rather than harsh self-criticism, particularly during difficult times.

1. **Practice Self-Kindness** Instead of berating yourself for mistakes, practice speaking to yourself as you would to a dear friend. Acknowledge your struggles without judgment and remind yourself that imperfection is part of being human.

2. **Embrace Common Humanity** Recognizing that suffering and setbacks are universal experiences fosters connection rather than isolation. Understanding that everyone faces difficulties helps build resilience and reduces feelings of self-pity.

3. **Mindful Self-Awareness** Self-compassion involves being present with your emotions without over-identifying with them. Mindfulness allows you to observe thoughts and feelings without being consumed by them, fostering a healthier emotional state.

4. **Develop Self-Soothing Techniques** Engaging in activities that provide comfort, whether it's listening to music, taking a walk, or engaging in creative expression, can help regulate emotions during tough times.

Daily Habits That Build Emotional Strength

Building emotional resilience is not a one-time effort but an ongoing practice. Incorporating the following daily habits strengthens the ability to navigate life's challenges with greater ease:

1. **Gratitude Practice.** Regularly reflecting on things to be grateful for shifts focus from what is lacking to what is present, fostering a more resilient mindset.

2. **Physical Movement.** Exercise is a powerful tool for emotional regulation. Physical activity releases endorphins, reduces stress hormones, and improves overall emotional well-being.

3. **Intentional Rest and Recovery.** Resilience does not mean relentless endurance. Prioritizing sleep, relaxation, and activities that replenish energy prevents burnout and enhances emotional strength.

4. **Journaling for Emotional Clarity.** Writing down thoughts and emotions helps process experiences and identify patterns in thinking. It serves as a therapeutic tool for self-reflection and problem-solving.

5. **Setting Healthy Boundaries.** Protecting time, energy, and mental space from unnecessary stressors is essential for maintaining resilience. Learning to say no to draining commitments and toxic relationships fosters emotional well-being.

6. **Engaging in Play and Laughter.** Playfulness and humor act as buffers against stress. Engaging in activities that bring joy and incorporating laughter into daily life strengthen emotional resilience and enhance overall well-being.

Final Thoughts

Emotional resilience is an evolving skill, not a fixed trait. It is cultivated through deliberate practices, mindset shifts, and self-care habits. The ability to remain composed under pressure, embrace change, practice self-compassion, and engage in resilience-building habits empowers individuals to navigate life's challenges with greater ease. Just like astronauts train their minds to endure the vast unknown of space, we, too, can train ourselves to face uncertainty with courage and adaptability. Resilience is not just about bouncing back; it's about moving forward, stronger than before.

CHAPTER 4

MASTERING YOUR FOCUS

D id you know that the average human attention span has decreased from 12 seconds in the year 2000 to just 8 seconds today, shorter than that of a goldfish? In an age of endless notifications, multitasking, and digital distractions, mastering focus has become one of the most valuable skills for personal and professional success. The ability to direct attention with precision, sustain concentration for extended periods, and tune out distractions is not just a trait of the highly productive it is an art that can be cultivated and refined.

The Psychology of Attention and Concentration

Focus is not merely about willpower; it is a complex cognitive process governed by the brain's attentional systems. Attention is controlled by networks within the prefrontal cortex, which helps regulate what we choose to concentrate on and what we filter out. Neuroscientists distinguish between two primary types of attention:

1. **Selective Attention** – The ability to focus on one task while ignoring competing stimuli. This is the kind of focus required when reading a book in a noisy café or working on a project despite incoming messages.

2. **Sustained Attention** – The capacity to maintain focus over long periods, crucial for deep work, learning, and productivity.

Both forms of attention are influenced by external factors (such as environment and distractions) and internal factors (such as mood, motivation, and mental fatigue). Understanding how attention works allows us to harness its power and direct it effectively.

Identifying and Eliminating Distractions

Distractions are the enemy of focus, and they come in many forms: digital interruptions, environmental noise, internal thoughts, and multitasking habits. The first step in mastering focus is recognizing these obstacles and implementing strategies to minimize them.

1. **Digital Detox** – Notifications from emails, social media, and instant messaging can fragment attention. Using focus modes, turning off non-essential alerts, or setting designated "deep work" hours can significantly improve concentration.

2. **Optimizing Your Environment** – The physical space in which you work, or study plays a crucial role in sustaining attention. A clutter-free workspace, noise-canceling headphones, or a dedicated quiet area can reduce environmental distractions.

3. **Understanding the Cost of Multitasking** – While it may seem efficient, multitasking actually reduces cognitive performance. Studies show that switching between tasks can lower productivity by up to 40%. Training yourself to

focus on one task at a time enhances efficiency and mental clarity.

4. **Managing Internal Distractions** – Anxiety, stress, and intrusive thoughts can pull attention away from the task at hand. Journaling before work, setting clear intentions, and practicing mindfulness can help mitigate internal disruptions.

Training Your Brain for Deep Work and Sustained Focus

Deep work, a term popularized by Cal Newport, refers to the ability to focus intensely on cognitively demanding tasks without distractions. Training your brain for deep work requires structured practice and intentional habits.

1. **Time Blocking** – Allocating specific blocks of time for focused work prevents distractions and promotes consistency. For example, scheduling 90-minute work sessions with short breaks enhances sustained attention.

2. **The Pomodoro Technique** – A method that involves working in 25-minute bursts with 5-minute breaks in between. This prevents mental fatigue and keeps focus sharp.

3. **Developing a Pre-Work Routine** – Engaging in a ritual before deep work, such as meditating, reviewing goals, or taking a few deep breaths, signals to the brain that it's time to focus.

4. **Cognitive Endurance Training** – Just like physical exercise strengthens muscles, mental endurance can be built by gradually increasing the length of focused work sessions.

5. **Eliminating the Need for Willpower** – Instead of relying on self-control, creating structured habits such as setting a strict start time for deep work reduces the mental effort required to maintain focus.

The Power of Mindfulness in Improving Mental Clarity

Mindfulness, the practice of maintaining present-moment awareness without judgment, is a powerful tool for enhancing focus. Neuroscientific research shows that mindfulness improves cognitive flexibility, emotional regulation, and attention span.

1. **Mindful Breathing** – Taking slow, deliberate breaths increases oxygen flow to the brain and enhances concentration.

2. **Observation Exercises** – Spending a few minutes observing an object or surroundings with full attention strengthens the ability to focus.

3. **Body Scanning** – Bringing awareness to physical sensations helps anchor the mind and reduces mental distractions.

4. **Mindful Breaks** – Instead of checking emails or social media, using breaks to engage in mindful activities such as stretching or stepping outside refreshes the mind for better focus.

5. **Gratitude and Reflection** – Ending the day with reflection and gratitude practices enhances mental clarity and reduces stress, which can otherwise fragment attention.

Simple Exercises to Sharpen Attention and Memory

Developing a razor-sharp focus is a skill that improves with practice. Below are practical exercises designed to strengthen concentration and memory:

1. **The 5-Minute Focus Drill** – Choose a simple object (such as a candle flame or a ticking clock) and focus on it for five minutes without letting your mind wander. Gradually increase the duration.

2. **Memory Association Games** – Creating mental connections between new information and existing knowledge enhances recall and strengthens attention to detail.

3. **Reading with Full Presence** – When reading, avoid skimming and instead absorb each sentence with full engagement. Summarizing what you've read afterwards further solidifies retention.

4. **Counting Backwards by Sevens** – A simple mental exercise that requires concentration and strengthens cognitive endurance.

5. **Visualization Techniques** – Mentally rehearsing tasks before performing them sharpens focus and primes the brain for success.

6. **Single-Task Challenges** – Assign yourself a daily task that requires undivided attention, such as cooking a meal without distractions or solving a puzzle without interruptions.

Final Thoughts

Mastering focus is not about eliminating distractions entirely but about developing the discipline to navigate them effectively. By understanding the psychology of attention, eliminating common distractions, training for deep work, practicing mindfulness, and engaging in focus-enhancing exercises, anyone can strengthen their ability to concentrate. In a world full of competing demands for our attention, the ability to focus deeply is not just an advantage; it is a superpower.

CHAPTER 5

OVERCOMING SELF-DOUBT AND FEAR

D id you know that some of the world's most successful people, from Albert Einstein to Oprah Winfrey, struggled with self-doubt? Despite their incredible achievements, they often felt like frauds or feared failure. This phenomenon, commonly known as imposter syndrome, plagues millions of people. However, the key to their success wasn't the absence of self-doubt. It was their ability to overcome it.

Understanding the Roots of Fear and Self-Criticism

Fear and self-doubt don't appear out of thin air. They have deep-seated origins, often stemming from past experiences, societal conditioning, or personal insecurities. Understanding where these feelings come from is the first step to conquering them.

For many, self-doubt originates in childhood. Perhaps you were criticized for making mistakes or compared to others who seemed more talented, intelligent, or capable. Over time, these external voices can become internalized, forming what psychologists call the "inner critic."

On the other hand, fear is an evolutionary mechanism designed to protect us. Our ancestors relied on fear to survive in the wild, avoiding potential threats. Today, however, fear often takes the form of psychological barriers, such as fear of failure, rejection, or the unknown, rather than physical dangers.

Unfortunately, our brains are wired to prioritize negative experiences over positive ones, a phenomenon known as negativity bias. This means that self-critical thoughts tend to dominate, making it easy to dwell on past failures rather than future possibilities. Recognizing that fear and self-doubt are natural responses rather than truths about our abilities can help us take the first step toward change.

How to Silence Your Inner Critic

Your inner critic is like an unwelcome guest at a dinner party, always ready to point out your flaws and mistakes but never offering anything constructive. The good news? You don't have to listen to it.

The first step to silencing your inner critic is awareness. Pay attention to your negative self-talk and challenge its validity. Ask yourself:

- Would I say this to a close friend?
- Is there actual evidence that supports this thought?
- Am I overgeneralizing or catastrophizing the situation?

Once you start questioning the validity of these negative thoughts, they begin to lose their power. Another effective strategy is to replace self-critical statements with compassionate ones. Instead of saying, "I'm terrible at public speaking," try, "I'm still learning, and every attempt makes me better."

Additionally, using mindfulness techniques such as meditation can help you distance yourself from your thoughts rather than being consumed by them. By practicing self-awareness and self-compassion, you can turn down the volume on your inner critic and create space for confidence to grow.

Shifting from a Fixed Mindset to a Growth Mindset

One of the most powerful ways to overcome self-doubt is by shifting from a fixed mindset to a growth mindset. A fixed mindset believes that intelligence, talent, and abilities are static traits; you either have them, or you don't. A growth mindset, on the other hand, recognizes that skills and abilities can be developed with effort and perseverance.

Dr. Carol Dweck, a leading psychologist, conducted extensive research on the impact of mindset. She found that individuals with a growth mindset are more resilient, embrace challenges, and view failures as opportunities to learn rather than evidence of their limitations.

To cultivate a growth mindset:

1. **Reframe Failure** – See setbacks as learning experiences rather than signs of incompetence.

2. **Adopt the Word "Yet"** – Instead of saying, "I can't do this," say, "I can't do this yet."

3. **Embrace Effort** – Understand that mastery comes from consistent effort, not innate talent.

4. **Seek Constructive Feedback** – View criticism as an opportunity to improve rather than a personal attack.

By shifting your perspective, you can transform self-doubt into self-improvement, turning obstacles into steppingstones toward success.

Small Confidence-Building Actions That Create Momentum

Confidence isn't something you either have or don't have; it's something you build. And like a muscle, confidence grows stronger with consistent exercise. The key is to start small and build momentum over time.

1. **Set and Achieve Small Goals** – Confidence comes from achievement. Start with small, manageable tasks that give you a sense of accomplishment. Whether it's speaking up in a meeting or trying a new hobby, small wins add up.

2. **Celebrate Progress** – Too often, we focus on how far we have to go rather than how far we've come. Take time to acknowledge and celebrate your progress, no matter how small.

3. **Step Outside Your Comfort Zone** – Growth happens outside of comfort zones. Challenge yourself to do something slightly uncomfortable every day, whether it's initiating a conversation with a stranger or tackling a new challenge at work.

4. **Practice Positive Affirmations** – The way you talk to yourself matters. Affirmations like "I am capable," "I am resilient," and "I am enough" can help shift your mindset and reinforce positive beliefs.

5. **Improve Your Posture and Body Language** – Research shows that adopting a confident posture (such as standing tall with shoulders back) can actually increase feelings of confidence. Small changes in body language can have a big impact on your mindset.

Each small action builds upon the last, creating a snowball effect that strengthens confidence over time. By consistently stepping forward, no matter how small the steps, self-doubt begins to fade.

How to Embrace Discomfort and Take Calculated Risks

Growth requires discomfort. If you never push beyond what feels safe, you'll never discover what you're truly capable of. The most successful individuals understand that discomfort is not something to avoid—it's something to embrace.

1. **Redefine Fear as Excitement** – Physiologically, fear and excitement produce similar responses in the body (increased heart rate, adrenaline rush). By reframing nervousness as excitement, you can shift your mindset from avoidance to action.

2. **Take Small, Calculated Risks** – Overcoming fear doesn't mean making reckless decisions. It means taking smart risks that push you forward. Start with low-stakes risks, such as sharing an idea in a group setting, then gradually take on bigger challenges.

3. **Develop a "What's the Worst That Could Happen?" Mindset** – Often, we overestimate the consequences of failure. Ask yourself, "What's the worst that could happen?" and "How would I handle it?" You'll likely realize that even the worst-case scenario is manageable.

4. **Build Resilience Through Exposure** – The more you expose yourself to discomfort, the less intimidating it becomes. If public speaking scares you, start by speaking in front of a mirror, then to a small group, then to a larger audience.

5. **Surround Yourself with Supportive People** – Fear thrives in isolation. Surrounding yourself with encouraging and like-minded individuals can help you gain the confidence to take risks and pursue your goals.

Ultimately, self-doubt and fear are part of the human experience. But they don't have to control your life. By understanding their origins, silencing your inner critic, adopting a growth mindset, taking small confidence-building actions, and embracing discomfort, you can break free from the limitations they impose. The path to success isn't about eliminating fear; it's about moving forward in spite of it.

CULTIVATING POSITIVITY IN DAILY LIFE

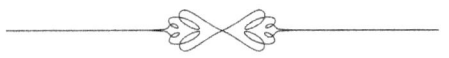

D id you know that practicing gratitude can actually rewire your brain? Neuroscientific research suggests that regularly expressing gratitude strengthens neural pathways associated with happiness and reduces activity in areas linked to stress and anxiety. Imagine that a simple "thank you" has the power to reshape your mindset and improve your overall well-being. The pursuit of positivity is not about ignoring challenges or forcing a constant state of cheerfulness; rather, it is about cultivating habits that allow joy, resilience, and fulfillment to naturally flourish in your life. This chapter explores the transformative power of positiveness in daily life, from the science of gratitude to the subtle magic of everyday moments.

The Science of Gratitude and Its Impact on Mental Health

Gratitude is more than just a polite gesture; it is a fundamental psychological tool that enhances well-being. Research in positive psychology has revealed that individuals who practice gratitude consistently experience lower levels of stress and depression. Studies have shown that keeping a gratitude journal, in which you jot down a few things you're thankful for daily, can lead to lasting improvements in mood and even physical health. The reason behind this is fascinating: gratitude activates the brain's reward system, increasing dopamine and serotonin levels, two key neurotransmitters responsible for happiness.

Furthermore, gratitude enhances resilience. People who regularly acknowledge the good in their lives are better equipped to cope with adversity. A study conducted by the University of California, Berkeley, found that individuals who wrote letters of gratitude experienced significant improvements in their mental health, even weeks after completing the exercise. The simple act of reflecting on positive aspects of life shifts the focus away from negativity, making challenges seem more manageable.

Finding Beauty and Meaning in Ordinary Moments

Life is filled with moments that, at first glance, may appear mundane. However, a shift in perception can reveal their hidden beauty and significance. Consider the warmth of the morning sun on your face, the rhythmic sound of rain tapping against the window, or the genuine smile of a stranger passing by. These small moments hold the potential to bring immense joy if only we take the time to notice them.

Practicing mindfulness is one way to cultivate an appreciation for ordinary experiences. By fully immersing yourself in the present moment, you develop a deeper awareness of your surroundings and emotions. For instance, instead of rushing through your morning coffee, take a moment to savor its aroma and warmth. Instead of viewing a routine walk as just another task, appreciate the movement of your body and the details of your environment. When you train yourself to find beauty in the everyday, life feels richer and more meaningful.

Another way to uncover meaning in daily life is by engaging in small acts of kindness. A simple gesture, like helping a neighbor carry grocery or sending an encouraging message to a friend, can transform an otherwise ordinary day into a moment of deep fulfillment. The ripple effect of kindness not only uplifts others but also reinforces a sense of purpose in your own life.

How to Surround Yourself with Uplifting Influences

The company you keep has a profound impact on your mindset and emotional health. Just as negativity can be contagious, so can positivity. Surrounding yourself with uplifting influences, whether in the form of people, media, or environments, plays a crucial role in shaping your outlook on life.

One way to cultivate a supportive social circle is by seeking out relationships that inspire and uplift you. This does not mean cutting off individuals who are struggling, but rather, finding a balance that allows for mutual support and encouragement. Spending time with optimistic, growth-oriented people can help reinforce your own positive habits and perspectives.

Beyond personal relationships, the content you consume daily also shapes your thoughts and emotions. Take a moment to assess your media intake. Are you regularly exposed to negative news, toxic social media discussions, or entertainment that drains your energy? While staying informed is important, curating a more positive media diet can significantly enhance your mood. This could mean following uplifting podcasts, reading books that inspire you, or engaging with social media accounts that promote encouragement and personal growth.

Your physical environment also plays a role in your well-being. A cluttered, chaotic space can contribute to stress, whereas an organized and aesthetically pleasing environment can promote a sense of calm and happiness. Simple changes, like adding plants to your home, displaying personal photos, or incorporating elements of nature, can make a significant difference in fostering positivity.

Developing a Habit of Positive Self-Talk

The way you speak to yourself shapes your self-perception and overall mindset. Many people unknowingly engage in negative self-talk, which can lead to self-doubt and diminished confidence. The good news is that, with practice, you can replace self-criticism with self-compassion and encouragement.

A powerful technique to develop positive self-talk is cognitively reframing challenging negative thoughts and replacing them with constructive perspectives. For example, instead of saying, "I always mess things up," try, "I am still learning, and mistakes are a part of growth." Instead of "I am not good enough," affirm, "I am capable and improving every day." By consciously shifting your internal dialogue, you create a more supportive and motivating mental environment.

Another effective approach is using affirmations and positive statements that reinforce your strengths and values. Repeating affirmations daily, such as "I am resilient," "I deserve happiness," or "I am worthy of love and success," helps rewire your subconscious mind to embrace a more positive self-view. Writing these affirmations down or placing them where you can see them regularly can reinforce their impact.

Transforming Small Daily Routines into Sources of Joy

Often, we associate happiness with major milestones— vacations, promotions, or special celebrations. However, true joy is often found in the seemingly insignificant moments of everyday life. By approaching daily routines with intention and mindfulness, you can turn even the most ordinary tasks into sources of happiness.

Start by identifying small rituals that bring you comfort. This could be lighting a scented candle while reading, listening to music while cooking, or taking a few deep breaths before starting your day. These small actions, when done with awareness and appreciation, become anchors of positivity throughout your day.

Adding a creative element to your routine can also elevate daily experiences. If you typically go for a walk, consider taking a different route to explore new scenery. If you enjoy cooking, experiment with new flavors and recipes. Infusing creativity into routine tasks brings a sense of novelty and excitement to everyday life.

Finally, take time to celebrate small wins. Whether it's completing a task you've been putting off, making progress toward a goal, or simply showing kindness to someone, acknowledging these moments reinforces a sense of accomplishment and fulfillment.

Final Thoughts

Cultivating positivity in daily life is not about ignoring difficulties but about intentionally focusing on the aspects of life that bring joy, meaning, and inspiration. Through gratitude, mindfulness, uplifting influences, positive self-talk, and joyful routines, you can create a life rich in optimism and resilience. The beauty of positivity is that it is self-sustaining; the more you nurture it, the more it grows, brightening not only your own life but also the lives of those around you.

EMOTIONAL INTELLIGENCE FOR A FULFILLING LIFE

The Secret Ingredient to Success and Happiness

Did you know that emotional intelligence (EQ) is a better predictor of success than IQ? Studies show that people with high emotional intelligence are more likely to thrive in relationships, careers, and overall well-being. Unlike intelligence quotient (IQ), which remains relatively stable throughout life, EQ can be developed and improved over time. It acts as an invisible force shaping our interactions, decisions, and personal growth.

Imagine walking into a room where two people are in a heated debate. One person raises their voice and becomes defensive, while the other remains calm, listens intently, and responds with understanding. The latter likely possesses high emotional intelligence, a trait that not only helps in conflict resolution but also in maintaining strong relationships and mental peace. But what exactly is emotional intelligence, and why does it matter so much?

Understanding Emotional Intelligence and Why It Matters

Emotional intelligence refers to the ability to recognize, understand, manage, and influence emotions, both our own and those of others. Coined by psychologist Daniel Goleman, EQ consists of five key components:

1. **Self-awareness** – Understanding one's emotions and how they affect thoughts and behavior.

2. **Self-regulation** – The ability to manage emotions in a healthy and constructive manner.

3. **Motivation** – Harnessing emotions to achieve personal and professional goals.

4. **Empathy** – Recognizing and understanding the emotions of others.

5. **Social skills** – Navigating social interactions effectively and harmoniously.

People with high EQ tend to experience greater career success, improved relationships, and enhanced emotional well-being. They are better equipped to handle stress, make sound decisions, and cultivate meaningful connections with others.

Managing Emotions in Relationships and Social Settings

Our emotions act as both guides and barriers in our interactions. Managing them effectively can strengthen relationships, while mismanaging them can lead to misunderstandings and conflict.

Recognizing Emotional Triggers

Emotions can be unpredictable, and certain situations or words may trigger strong reactions. Recognizing these triggers is the first step to mastering emotional regulation. Ask yourself:

- What situations make me feel anxious, angry, or frustrated?

- How do I typically react in these situations?
- Can I reframe my perspective to respond more effectively?

The Power of Pause

When emotions run high, taking a moment before responding can make a significant difference. A simple technique is the **"pause and breathe"** method:

1. **Pause** – Take a deep breath before reacting.
2. **Assess** – Consider your emotions and what triggered them.
3. **Respond** – Choose a response that aligns with your values and long-term goals.

Practicing this technique can prevent emotional outbursts and improve interactions in both personal and professional relationships.

The Importance of Empathy and How to Develop It

Empathy is the ability to understand and share the feelings of another person. It is a cornerstone of emotional intelligence and plays a crucial role in building trust, resolving conflicts, and fostering meaningful relationships.

Types of Empathy

1. **Cognitive Empathy** – Understanding another person's perspective without necessarily feeling their emotions.
2. **Emotional Empathy** – Feeling what the other person is experiencing.

3. **Compassionate Empathy** – A combination of understanding and feeling emotions, leading to a desire to help.

How to Cultivate Empathy

- **Active Listening** – Instead of formulating your response while someone is talking, truly focus on their words, tone, and body language.

- **Ask Open-Ended Questions** – Encourage others to share their feelings and thoughts by asking questions like, "How did that make you feel?"

- **Practice Perspective-Taking** – Imagine yourself in the other person's situation to better understand their emotions.

- **Engage in Acts of Kindness** – Small gestures of support or encouragement can enhance your ability to empathize with others.

Empathy fosters deeper connections and helps us navigate social settings with sensitivity and understanding.

How to Communicate Effectively While Maintaining Emotional Balance

Effective communication is not just about speaking; it's about connecting. High-EQ individuals communicate in a way that fosters clarity, understanding, and emotional harmony.

Key Principles of Emotionally Intelligent Communication

1. **Self-awareness in Communication**
   o Pay attention to your tone, facial expressions, and body language.

- o Be mindful of how your emotions influence your words.

2. **Emotional Regulation During Conversations**
   - o If you feel overwhelmed, take a deep breath before responding.
   - o Avoid reacting impulsively to negative emotions.

3. **Assertive Yet Respectful Speech**
   - o Use "I" statements to express yourself without blaming others (e.g., "I feel hurt when..." instead of "You always...").
   - o Maintain a calm and composed tone.

4. **Nonverbal Communication Awareness**
   - o Over 70% of communication is nonverbal, pay attention to facial expressions, eye contact, and gestures.

5. **The Art of Listening**
   - o Show genuine interest by nodding, maintaining eye contact, and summarizing key points.
   - o Avoid interrupting and let the other person express themselves fully.

By mastering these skills, you can navigate conversations more effectively and build stronger, more positive relationships.

Resolving Conflicts with a Calm and Rational Mindset

Conflict is inevitable, but emotional intelligence can turn conflicts into opportunities for growth and understanding. The key lies in managing emotions and approaching disagreements with a rational mindset.

Steps to Resolving Conflict Effectively

1. **Stay Calm** – A heated reaction escalates conflict. Take deep breaths and ground yourself before responding.

2. **Listen Actively** – Understand the other person's perspective without immediately defending your own.

3. **Acknowledge Emotions** – Validate the other person's feelings to show empathy and build trust.

4. **Find Common Ground** – Identify shared goals or values to foster a cooperative mindset.

5. **Focus on Solutions** – Instead of dwelling on the problem, work together to find a resolution that benefits both parties.

6. **Know When to Walk Away** – If emotions are too high, it's okay to take a break and revisit the conversation later.

Conflict resolution is not about winning or losing but about understanding and finding balance.

Final Thoughts: The Lifelong Journey of Emotional Intelligence

Emotional intelligence is not a destination but an ongoing journey. By becoming more aware of your emotions, practicing empathy, communicating effectively, and resolving conflicts with a calm mindset, you can significantly enhance your personal and professional life.

In a world where technology often dominates interactions, emotional intelligence remains one of the most valuable skills a person can develop. It leads to deeper connections, greater success, and a more fulfilling life.

So, as you move forward, remember that, mastering emotional intelligence is not about suppressing emotions but about understanding, managing, and using them as tools for growth and connection. The more you invest in developing your EQ, the richer and more rewarding your life will become.

THE POWER OF VISUALIZATION AND AFFIRMATIONS

Did you know that Olympic athletes often spend as much time training their minds as they do their bodies? In fact, studies have shown that mentally rehearsing a physical activity can activate the same neural pathways as actually performing the movement. This incredible phenomenon highlights the power of visualization, a tool that can shape reality through the subconscious mind, drive motivation, and reinforce a positive mindset. When paired with affirmations, visualization becomes even more potent, allowing individuals to reprogram their thoughts and cultivate self-belief.

How Visualization Shapes Reality Through the Subconscious Mind

The subconscious mind is a vast reservoir of potential, absorbing thoughts, beliefs, and emotions that ultimately dictate behavior. Unlike the conscious mind, which engages in logical reasoning and critical thinking, the subconscious does not distinguish between real and imagined experiences. This is why visualization is so effective; by consistently picturing a desired outcome, individuals condition their minds to perceive that goal as achievable, even inevitable.

Neurologically, visualization works by activating the brain's reticular activating system (RAS), a network of neurons that filters information and determines what is most important. When you focus on a specific vision repeatedly, the RAS tunes in to opportunities aligned with that vision. This explains why, after deciding to buy a particular car model, you suddenly start seeing it everywhere your mind has been primed to notice it. Similarly, visualizing success or confidence prompts the subconscious to seek out reinforcing experiences and behaviors.

Furthermore, the brain cannot differentiate between vividly imagined experiences and real ones. Studies in sports psychology demonstrate that athletes who engage in mental rehearsal show significant improvement in performance, often compared to those who physically train. This principle applies beyond athletics, aiding in academic achievement, career success, and personal growth. By envisioning yourself excelling in a situation, you create a mental blueprint that your subconscious follows.

Techniques for Creating Mental Imagery That Fuels Motivation

The effectiveness of visualization depends on clarity, repetition, and emotional engagement. To maximize its impact, employ the following techniques:

1. Vivid Sensory Engagement

Engage all five senses when visualizing. Instead of merely seeing an image in your mind, feel the textures, hear the sounds, and even smell the surroundings. For example, if you are visualizing yourself delivering a powerful speech, imagine the warmth of the stage lights, the sound of applause, and the confidence in your voice.

2. Future Self Visualization

Picture yourself in the future, having already achieved your goal. How do you look? How do you carry yourself? What emotions are you experiencing? This practice reinforces self-identity as a successful individual and aligns your subconscious beliefs with your aspirations.

3. Mental Rehearsal for Specific Situations

Before facing a challenge, mentally walk through the scenario. If preparing for a job interview, visualize yourself answering questions with ease, maintaining strong posture, and establishing rapport. This primes your brain to perform in alignment with your mental script.

4. Vision Boards for Reinforcement

Creating a physical representation of your goals through a vision board helps reinforce your visualization. Fill it with images, words, and symbols that represent your aspirations. Place it where you will see it daily to continually reinforce your focus.

5. Daily Visualization Sessions

Dedicate a few minutes each day to focused visualization. Morning sessions can set a positive tone for the day, while evening sessions reinforce progress and intentions. Consistency is key; the more frequently you visualize, the more deeply ingrained these mental images become.

Crafting Personalized Affirmations That Reinforce Positivity

Affirmations are powerful statements designed to challenge and overcome self-doubt. When repeated regularly, they help rewire the subconscious mind by replacing negative beliefs with positive, empowering ones. The key to effective affirmations lies in personalization, present-tense phrasing, and emotional conviction.

1. Structure Affirmations in the Present Tense

Instead of saying, "I will be confident," affirm, "I am confident and capable." The subconscious mind responds more effectively to present-tense statements, reinforcing the belief as an existing reality rather than a distant goal.

2. Use Positive Language

Avoid negative words. Rather than saying, "I am not afraid of failure," say, "I embrace challenges and grow from them." This ensures your focus remains on empowerment rather than fear.

3. Infuse Emotion and Conviction

The more emotion you attach to your affirmations, the more effective they become. Rather than mechanically repeating words, feel them deeply. Visualize the truth of the affirmation as you say it, engaging with the emotions of success and confidence.

4. Customize Affirmations for Specific Goals

Craft affirmations that align with your personal aspirations. If aiming for career advancement, say, "I am a skilled and valued professional, attracting new opportunities." If focusing on self-love, affirm, "I deeply respect and cherish myself."

5. Integrate Affirmations into Daily Life

Repeat affirmations during daily routines, such as: brushing your teeth, commuting, or exercising. Write them on sticky notes and place them in visible spots, like your mirror or workspace, as continuous reinforcement.

Using Guided Imagery to Enhance Confidence and Resilience

Guided imagery is a form of directed visualization where a narrative leads the mind through a specific scenario designed to evoke calmness, confidence, or resilience. This practice is particularly effective in overcoming anxiety, preparing for high-stakes situations, and fostering emotional strength.

1. Confidence-Boosting Visualization

Picture yourself excelling in a situation that typically makes you nervous. Whether it's public speaking, social interactions, or competitive sports, visualize success with rich detail. This primes your brain to associate confidence with that scenario.

2. Overcoming Fear Through Mental Mastery

For situations that evoke fear, mentally rehearse facing them with poise. If flying makes you anxious, visualize yourself boarding a plane, feeling calm, and enjoying the journey. This rewires your subconscious to associate relaxation rather than stress with the situation.

3. Resilience-Building Through Adversity Rehearsal

Imagine encountering a setback and responding with grace and determination. See yourself problem-solving, remaining composed, and ultimately succeeding. This strengthens resilience by training your mind to handle challenges with confidence.

How to Integrate Visualization into Daily Routines

To harness the full benefits of visualization, it must become a habitual practice woven into daily life. Here is simple yet effective ways to make it a natural part of your routine:

1. Morning Visualization Rituals

Start your day by visualizing a successful and fulfilling day ahead. Picture yourself navigating tasks with ease, interacting positively with others, and accomplishing your goals.

2. Visualization Before Sleep

End your day with a mental rehearsal of desired outcomes. Visualizing success before bed reinforces these images during sleep, a time when the subconscious is highly receptive to suggestion.

3. Pair Visualization with Meditation

Combine visualization with meditation for deeper focus. During meditation, vividly imagine your goals while in a relaxed state, allowing your subconscious to absorb them without distraction.

4. Use Visualization During Exercise

Engage in mental imagery while running, lifting weights, or practicing yoga. Picture your strength, endurance, and vitality growing with each movement, reinforcing positive beliefs about your physical abilities.

5. Leverage Micro-Visualization Moments

Take brief moments throughout the day to reinforce visualization. Whether waiting in line or pausing between tasks, use these snippets of time to mentally affirm your goals and visualize success.

Final Thoughts

Visualization and affirmations are not mere wishful thinking; they are powerful tools rooted in psychology and neuroscience. By consistently practicing mental imagery and positive affirmations, you reshape your subconscious mind, align your thoughts with your aspirations, and create an internal environment that fosters success. As Olympic athletes, high-achievers, and visionaries have demonstrated, the mind is a powerful ally when trained with intention. With dedication, you can harness its potential to manifest the life you envision.

CREATING A MINDSET FOR LONG-TERM HAPPINESS

D id you know that the human brain is wired for negativity? It's called the negativity bias; a survival mechanism that helped our ancestors avoid danger. While useful in the past, this tendency can make us chase fleeting pleasures instead of long-term fulfillment. The good news? We can rewire our thinking to cultivate lasting happiness.

Understanding the Difference Between Fleeting Pleasure and True Happiness

Happiness is often mistaken for pleasure, the momentary rush of joy from indulging in a favorite dessert, buying something new, or winning a game. These experiences trigger the brain's reward system, releasing dopamine, the "feel-good" neurotransmitter. However, this kind of happiness is short-lived, fading as soon as the moment passes. This explains why people constantly seek new thrills but remain dissatisfied.

True happiness, on the other hand, is deeper and more sustainable. It comes from a sense of purpose, meaningful relationships, personal growth, and living in alignment with one's values. Unlike fleeting pleasure, which is externally driven, true happiness is cultivated from within and can withstand life's inevitable ups and downs.

How to Distinguish Between the Two

Ask yourself these questions:

- Does this experience make me feel good only in the moment, or does it contribute to long-term well-being?
- Am I relying on external sources (e.g., material possessions, social validation) for my happiness?
- Will this choice enrich my life in a meaningful way over time? By shifting focus from momentary gratification to deeper fulfillment, we create a more stable and rewarding sense of happiness.

How to Align Daily Actions with Personal Values

Many people chase happiness in ways that contradict their core values. For instance, someone who values family might overwork themselves, missing out on time with loved ones. When actions misalign with values, it leads to inner conflict and dissatisfaction.

Steps to Align Actions with Values

1. **Identify Your Core Values:** Write down what matters most to you: family, health, creativity, service, growth, etc.

2. **Assess Your Current Actions:** Do your daily habits reflect your values? If not, what changes can you make?

3. **Set Intentional Goals:** Align goals with your values. If you value health, commit to regular exercise and nutritious eating. If you value connection, schedule quality time with loved ones.

4. **Make Decisions Based on Values:** Before making choices, ask: "Does this align with who I want to be?"

5. **Practice Self-Reflection:** Regularly check in with yourself to ensure your actions remain in harmony with your values.

When life is guided by values, fulfillment naturally follows. Each day feels more purposeful, reducing stress and regret.

Building Habits That Sustain Long-Term Fulfillment

Happiness isn't about one-time actions; it's built on consistent habits. Developing routines that promote well-being creates a foundation for sustained joy.

Key Habits for Lasting Happiness

1. **Gratitude Practice:** Reflect daily on what you appreciate. This shift focusses from what's missing to what's abundant.

2. **Mindfulness and Meditation:** Being present reduces stress and increases contentment.

3. **Physical Activity:** Exercise releases endorphins and promotes mental well-being.

4. **Healthy Social Connections:** Invest in deep, meaningful relationships rather than superficial interactions.

5. **Acts of Kindness:** Helping others boosts happiness and fosters a sense of purpose.

6. **Continuous Learning:** Personal growth keeps life engaging and fulfilling.

7. **Self-Care and Rest:** Prioritizing mental and physical health ensures sustainable energy for long-term happiness.

Creating small, intentional changes in daily routines leads to profound improvements in overall happiness.

The Importance of Purpose and Meaning in Life Satisfaction

Research shows that people with a strong sense of purpose live longer, healthier, and happier lives. Purpose gives direction, making challenges easier to navigate. Without meaning, even success can feel empty.

Finding Your Purpose

1. **Reflect on What Brings You Joy:** Identify activities that make you feel alive and fulfilled.

2. **Consider How You Can Serve Others:** Many find meaning in helping others, whether through career, volunteer work, or simple daily interactions.

3. **Explore Your Strengths:** Leverage your talents in ways that contribute to something bigger than yourself.

4. **Set Purpose-Driven Goals:** Align ambitions with what truly matters to you.

5. **Stay Open to Change:** Purpose can evolve over time. Be willing to adapt as you grow.

A meaningful life provides resilience, making difficulties feel like part of a greater journey rather than mere obstacles.

How to Develop an Inner State of Peace and Contentment

External circumstances fluctuate, but inner peace can remain constant. Contentment comes from within, independent of success, possessions, or recognition.

Practices to Cultivate Inner Peace

1. **Accept Imperfection:** Perfectionism fuels stress and dissatisfaction. Embrace flaws and mistakes as part of growth.

2. **Let Go of Comparison:** Social comparisons drain joy. Focus on your unique path.

3. **Detach from Materialism:** True happiness isn't found in possessions but in experiences and relationships.

4. **Practice Forgiveness:** Holding onto grudges creates inner turmoil. Letting go fosters peace.

5. **Engage in Mindfulness:** Stay present instead of dwelling on the past or worrying about the future.

6. **Develop Self-Compassion:** Treat yourself with kindness, just as you would a friend.

7. **Simplify Life:** Too many commitments lead to overwhelm. Prioritize what truly matters.

By mastering inner contentment, happiness becomes a steady state rather than something dependent on external factors.

Conclusion

True happiness isn't found in fleeting pleasures but in purposeful living, aligned actions, and sustainable habits. By prioritizing values, fostering meaningful relationships, and cultivating inner peace, we create a mindset for lifelong fulfillment. The path to happiness isn't about chasing highs; it's about building a life that feels rich and meaningful every day.

DESIGNING YOUR MENTAL AND EMOTIONAL MASTERY PLAN

The Power of Mastery: Your Personalized Blueprint for a Stronger Mind

Did you know that some of the greatest minds in history, Leonardo da Vinci, Albert Einstein, and even modern icons like Oprah Winfrey, have followed structured mental and emotional mastery plans? These individuals didn't just rely on talent or luck; they cultivated habits and routines that strengthened their minds and emotional resilience. Now, it's your turn to do the same.

Mastering your mind and emotions is a lifelong journey, and like any successful endeavor, it requires a structured plan. In this chapter, we'll dive into how to integrate various techniques into a cohesive system, develop a sustainable mental wellness routine, track your progress, overcome setbacks, and stay committed to continuous growth.

Integrating Techniques into a Personalized System

Over the previous chapters, you've explored numerous techniques to enhance your mental and emotional well-being. But how do you merge them into a plan tailored to your unique needs? Here's a step-by-step approach:

1. Assess Your Core Needs

Before you start, take stock of your mental and emotional strengths and weaknesses. Ask yourself:

- What are my primary mental struggles (e.g., anxiety, stress, procrastination)?
- What techniques have resonated with me the most?
- Where do I need the most growth?

By identifying these key areas, you can prioritize techniques that address your specific needs.

2. Select Your Core Techniques

Not all strategies work for everyone, and that's okay. Choose techniques that align with your lifestyle and preferences. Here are a few categories to consider:

- **Mindfulness & Meditation:** Breathing exercises, guided meditation, and present-moment awareness.
- **Cognitive Techniques:** Thought reframing, gratitude journaling, and positive affirmations.
- **Emotional Regulation Strategies:** Journaling, practicing self-compassion, and using relaxation techniques.
- **Physical Well-Being:** Exercise, proper nutrition, and sleep hygiene.
- **Social & Environmental Factors:** Setting boundaries, surrounding yourself with positive influences, and engaging in fulfilling activities.

Select at least one strategy from each category to create a well-rounded system.

3. Structure Your Plan

Once you've selected techniques, organize them into a clear system. This can be done by dividing them into **daily, weekly, and emergency** routines:

Daily Practices:

- Morning meditation (5-10 minutes)
- Setting daily intentions
- Practicing gratitude (journaling or verbal)
- Physical movement (exercise, stretching, or yoga)
- Mindful breaks throughout the day

Weekly Practices:

- Reflecting on emotional patterns
- Engaging in creative or relaxing activities
- Social connection (calls, meetups, or support groups)
- Deep journaling or self-reflection exercises

Emergency Practices (for tough times):

- Deep breathing exercises for stress
- Reframing negative thoughts
- Temporary unplugging (digital detox for a few hours)
- Speaking to a friend or therapist

By structuring your plan in this way, you ensure consistency while allowing flexibility for different situations.

Developing a Daily and Weekly Mental Wellness Routine

Consistency is the key to success, and establishing a routine makes your mental mastery plan effective. Here's how you can build routines that stick:

1. Start Small and Build Gradually

Trying to implement everything at once can be overwhelming. Instead, start with one or two small daily habits and gradually add more. For example, begin with a simple morning gratitude practice before expanding to meditation and reflection.

2. Anchor Habits to Existing Routines

Pair new mental wellness habits with something you already do daily. For instance:

- Meditate right after brushing your teeth in the morning.
- Reflect on your emotions while having your evening tea.
- Write in your gratitude journal before bedtime.

By attaching new habits to established ones, they become more automatic.

3. Prioritize Quality Over Quantity

Your routine doesn't have to be lengthy; even a few minutes of intentional practice each day can yield significant benefits. The goal is **consistency**, not perfection.

4. Create a Ritual Around Your Practices

Make your wellness habits something you look forward to. Set up a peaceful meditation space, use a beautifully designed journal, or listen to calming music during your relaxation exercises.

5. Schedule Check-Ins

Once a week, set aside time to assess your emotional state, track your progress, and make necessary adjustments. This reflection prevents stagnation and helps fine-tune your approach.

Tracking Progress and Making Adjustments

Without tracking progress, it's easy to lose motivation. Here's how you can ensure you stay on track:

1. Use a Journal or Mental Wellness App

Documenting your experiences can highlight patterns, successes, and areas needing improvement. Track:

- Mood fluctuations
- Stress levels
- Successes and setbacks
- The effectiveness of different techniques

2. Rate Your Mental State Regularly

A simple 1-10 rating of your emotional and mental state can provide insights into trends and progress over time.

3. Adapt Based on Your Needs

Your plan isn't set in stone. If a technique isn't working or becomes redundant, swap it for another. Flexibility is crucial to long-term success.

Overcoming Setbacks and Staying Committed

Setbacks are a natural part of growth. The key is **how** you respond to them.

1. Reframe Setbacks as Learning Experiences

Instead of seeing a missed meditation session or a stressful day as failure, view it as feedback. Ask:

- What triggered this setback?
- How can I prepare better next time?

2. Use Accountability Systems

Consider:

- Having an accountability partner
- Joining an online mental wellness community
- Setting reminders or alarms for important practices

3. Celebrate Small Wins

Recognize your progress, no matter how small. Reward yourself when you maintain consistency or successfully navigate a difficult situation.

4. Be Kind to Yourself

Perfection isn't the goal; progress is. Treat yourself with the same compassion you'd offer a friend struggling with self-improvement.

The Lifelong Journey of Mastering Your Mind and Emotions

Mastery isn't a destination; it's an ongoing journey. As you evolve, so will your needs and strategies. Regularly revisit your plan and adjust it to fit your current phase of life.

1. Keep Expanding Your Knowledge

Explore new books, courses, and techniques to deepen your understanding of emotional intelligence and mental resilience.

2. Share and Teach What You Learn

Helping others strengthens your own commitment to growth. Teach a friend or mentor someone struggling with their mental wellness.

3. Accept That Mastery Is a Lifelong Process

Even experts have off days. The key is to keep showing up, refining your strategies, and prioritizing your well-being.

Final Thoughts: Designing a Life of Resilience and Joy

By now, you have the tools to create your own mental and emotional mastery plan. With structure, commitment, and self-compassion, you can navigate life's challenges with clarity and resilience. Start small, stay consistent, and embrace the journey your best self awaits.

So, what's your first step today? Write it down, commit to it, and take action. Your mind and emotions are in your hands, making them your greatest allies.

CHAPTER 11

THE SUBCONSCIOUS MIND AND THE POWER OF EMOTIONS

The Subconscious Mind's Role in Daily Life

The Unseen Influence: A Childhood Memory

As a child, James always felt an inexplicable anxiety whenever he had to speak in front of his class. Despite being well-prepared, his heart would race, his palms would sweat, and his mind would go blank. It wasn't until much later in life that he traced this reaction back to a single incident—when he had mispronounced a word in kindergarten and the class had erupted in laughter. This trivial moment had embedded itself deep within his subconscious mind, influencing his emotions and reactions without his conscious awareness.

This anecdote highlights the immense power of the subconscious mind in shaping daily experiences. Our subconscious mind operates like an unseen script, directing behaviors, emotions, and thoughts with an influence far beyond what we consciously perceive.

How the Subconscious Differs from the Conscious Mind

The human mind consists of two major components: the conscious and the subconscious. The conscious mind is responsible for logical thinking, decision-making, and problem-solving. It is the part of our cognition that actively engages with the world, analyzing situations and making deliberate choices. However, it is limited in capacity and can only focus on a few things at a time.

In contrast, the subconscious mind functions beneath our awareness. It processes vast amounts of information simultaneously, storing memories, habits, and emotional responses. Unlike the conscious mind, which operates in a linear, logical manner, the subconscious is more associative, linking past experiences to present situations in ways that are often beyond our immediate comprehension. It is responsible for our automatic reactions, deeply held beliefs, and habitual behaviors.

The Way Beliefs and Past Experiences Influence Emotions

Beliefs are often formed in early childhood and become deeply ingrained in the subconscious. These beliefs can be empowering, such as a strong sense of self-worth, or limiting, leading to fears, doubts, and anxieties. For example, a child who is repeatedly told they are not good at math may internalize this belief, leading to anxiety around numbers and avoidance of mathematical tasks, even into adulthood.

Similarly, past experiences serve as a foundation for emotional responses. When faced with a new situation, the subconscious mind quickly searches its archives for similar past events. If a person has experienced rejection, for example, their subconscious may trigger fear or hesitation in social interactions, even if there is no real danger of rejection in the present.

The Link Between Thoughts and Automatic Reactions

Because the subconscious mind operates in the background, it often dictates how we react to different situations before we have had a chance to consciously process them. Consider the way someone flinches when they hear a loud noise. This response occurs before the person has consciously identified the sound. Similarly, emotional reactions like feeling anxious before a job interview or frustrated in traffic are often automatic and stem from subconscious programming.

Automatic reactions also manifest in relationships. If someone grew up in a household where anger was expressed through yelling, they might subconsciously associate anger with raised voices, causing them to react defensively even when no real threat exists. Recognizing these patterns allows individuals to reprogram their subconscious reactions, replacing fear-based responses with more constructive behaviors.

How Emotions Drive Decisions and Behavior

The Science Behind Emotions: Chemical and Neurological Processes

Emotions are not just abstract feelings; they are deeply rooted in physiological processes. The brain plays a crucial role in generating emotions, primarily through the limbic system, which includes structures like the amygdala, hippocampus, and hypothalamus. These areas work together to process emotional stimuli and dictate how we respond.

Neurotransmitters and hormones such as dopamine, serotonin, and cortisol influence our emotional states. Dopamine, often associated with pleasure and motivation, drives behaviors that lead to rewards. Serotonin helps regulate mood, while cortisol, known as the stress hormone, prepares the body for fight-or-flight responses.

Understanding the biochemical nature of emotions helps explain why certain feelings seem beyond our control. For instance, when someone experiences fear, the amygdala activates, triggering the release of adrenaline and increasing heart rate, preparing the body to respond to a perceived threat. This process happens instantaneously, often before the conscious mind has had time to evaluate the situation rationally.

Why Subconscious Patterns Dictate Emotional Responses

Since the subconscious mind stores past experiences and emotional associations, it significantly influences how we react to situations. These emotional patterns operate much like a program running in the background, dictating responses based on historical data rather than present reality.

For example, if someone has repeatedly faced criticism from authority figures, their subconscious may associate authority with negative emotions. Even in a different context, such as receiving constructive feedback from a supportive boss, they might still experience anxiety, feeling as though they are being judged or reprimanded.

Breaking free from these ingrained emotional patterns requires self-awareness and intentional effort. Techniques such as mindfulness, cognitive reframing, and exposure therapy can help rewire these subconscious associations, allowing individuals to respond to situations in healthier ways.

The Impact of Early Conditioning on Emotional Regulation

Emotional regulation, the ability to manage and respond to emotions effectively, is heavily shaped by early life experiences. Children learn how to regulate their emotions through interactions with caregivers. If a child grows up in a nurturing environment where emotions are validated and addressed constructively, they are more likely to develop strong emotional regulation skills.

Conversely, if a child experiences emotional neglect or unpredictable parental responses, they may struggle with emotional regulation later in life. For instance, someone who was often ignored when expressing sadness might suppress their emotions as an adult, struggling to articulate their needs in relationships.

Moreover, cultural, and societal influences play a role in emotional conditioning. In some cultures, expressing emotions openly is encouraged, while in others, emotional restraint is valued. These cultural norms shape how individuals perceive and manage their emotions.

By recognizing the impact of early conditioning, individuals can work toward developing healthier emotional responses. Practices such as journaling, therapy, and self-reflection can help uncover deep-seated emotional patterns and replace them with more constructive approaches.

Conclusion

The subconscious mind and emotions work in tandem to shape human behavior in profound ways. While the conscious mind allows for rational decision-making, the subconscious mind silently directs much of our emotional world based on past experiences and ingrained beliefs. Understanding these mechanisms empowers individuals to break free from automatic reactions, cultivate emotional intelligence, and make more intentional choices in life.

By acknowledging the role of the subconscious in emotional responses and decision-making, we open the door to greater self-awareness and personal growth. Through conscious effort, it is possible to reprogram limiting beliefs, develop healthier emotional patterns, and take control of one's own mind and behavior.

THE SUBCONSCIOUS MIND PROGRAMMING AND PATTERNS

The Power of Thought Programming

Did you know that your brain processes around 60,000 thoughts per day? That's forty-two thoughts per minute! What's even more fascinating is that approximately 80% of these thoughts tend to be repetitive, shaping our perceptions, emotions, and reality. This phenomenon underscores the incredible power of thought programming, the ability of our recurring thoughts to influence our mental and emotional states, and even our outcomes in life.

How Recurring Thoughts Shape Mental and Emotional States

The human brain is like a sophisticated computer, and thoughts serve as the programming code that determines how we operate. Recurring thoughts create neural pathways, which reinforce certain behaviors and emotional responses over time. When we repeatedly think about a particular idea, our brain strengthens the connections associated with that thought, making it more automatic. This can be both a blessing and a curse, depending on whether our recurring thoughts are empowering or destructive.

For example, individuals who frequently entertain thoughts of self-doubt often experience feelings of anxiety, low self-esteem, and hesitation when making decisions. Their brains become conditioned to react in ways that align with these negative thoughts, reinforcing a cycle of uncertainty and insecurity. On the other hand, those who consistently engage in positive self-affirmation and optimistic thinking develop a mindset that supports confidence, resilience, and proactive behavior.

Research in neuroscience has shown that thoughts directly impact the brain's chemical environment. Positive thoughts trigger the release of neurotransmitters like dopamine and serotonin, which contribute to feelings of happiness and motivation. Conversely, negative thought patterns can lead to an overproduction of cortisol, the stress hormone, which, when prolonged, can contribute to anxiety, depression, and even physical ailments such as heart disease.

The Self-Fulfilling Prophecy: Expectations and Reality

One of the most compelling illustrations of thought programming is the concept of the self-fulfilling prophecy. A self-fulfilling prophecy occurs when an individual's expectations, whether positive or negative, directly influence their actions and the outcome of their experiences. When someone believes in a particular outcome strongly enough, they subconsciously behave in ways that make that outcome more likely to materialize.

For instance, if a student believes they are bad at mathematics, they might approach math-related tasks with anxiety and low confidence. This leads to decreased effort, avoidance of practice, and ultimately, poor performance on tests, reinforcing their belief that they are indeed bad at math. On the contrary, a student who believes they are capable of excelling in math will put in more effort, seek help when needed, and persist through challenges, achieving better results.

This phenomenon is not limited to academics; it extends to various aspects of life, including career growth, relationships, and personal development. Consider the placebo effect, where patients experience real improvements in their health simply because they believe they are receiving effective treatment, even if the treatment is inactive. The brain, influenced by belief, sends signals to the body that trigger physiological changes, demonstrating just how powerful thought programming can be.

Case Studies of Individuals Who Reprogrammed Their Thinking for Success

There are countless stories of individuals who transformed their lives by consciously reprogramming their thoughts. One notable example is Jim Carrey, the renowned actor and comedian. Before achieving fame, Carrey wrote himself a check for $10 million for "acting services rendered" and postdated it for a future date. He carried the check in his wallet for years, visualizing success daily. Through perseverance and unwavering belief in his potential, he eventually landed a role that paid him exactly $10 million, bringing his vision to life.

Another example is Oprah Winfrey, who overcame extreme poverty and childhood trauma to become one of the most influential media moguls in the world. She attributes much of her success to her mindset and the conscious effort she made to change her thoughts from those of limitation to those of abundance and possibility.

Even in the field of athletics, thought programming plays a crucial role. Michael Phelps, the most decorated Olympian in history, used visualization techniques to mentally rehearse every race. He would imagine himself executing perfect strokes and winning medals. This mental preparation contributed significantly to his record-breaking success.

These stories highlight a powerful truth: when individuals take control of their thought patterns and consciously choose empowering beliefs, they can dramatically alter the course of their lives.

Overcoming Negative Mental Patterns

While the power of thought programming is evident, many people struggle with negative mental patterns that seem deeply ingrained. These patterns often develop from past experiences, societal conditioning, and subconscious beliefs. However, the good news is that with awareness and intentional effort, it is possible to break free from these cycles and cultivate a more positive and productive mindset.

Recognizing Subconscious Negative Loops

Negative mental loops operate much like a stuck record, replaying the same limiting beliefs and fears over and over again. Common negative loops include thoughts such as:

- "I'm not good enough."
- "Nothing ever goes right for me."
- "I always fail."
- "I'll never be happy."

These thoughts become automatic responses to challenges, reinforcing a sense of helplessness and self-doubt. The first step in overcoming them is awareness. Keeping a thought journal can be an effective way to identify recurring negative patterns. By writing down your thoughts throughout the day, you can begin to notice trends and pinpoint which beliefs are holding you back.

Identifying Triggers That Lead to Emotional Distress

Negative thought patterns are often triggered by specific situations, environments, or interactions. Identifying these triggers is crucial to breaking the cycle. Some common triggers include:

- Social comparison: Constantly comparing oneself to others can lead to feelings of inadequacy and self-criticism.

- Fear of failure: Past experiences of failure can create anxiety about taking risks or trying new things.

- Negative self-talk: Inner dialogue that is overly critical can reinforce feelings of unworthiness.

- Unresolved trauma: Painful past experiences can manifest as recurring fears and doubts.

Once you have identified your triggers, you can begin developing strategies to counteract them. For instance, if social media triggers self-doubt, taking breaks from these platforms or curating a feed that promotes positivity can help.

Steps to Begin Shifting Ingrained Mental Habits

Changing thought patterns requires consistent effort and practice. Here are some effective steps to begin shifting ingrained negative habits:

1. **Practice Cognitive Reframing** – Challenge negative thoughts by reframing them in a more constructive way. Instead of thinking, "I'll never succeed," replace it with, "Success takes time, and I am learning and improving every day."

2. **Use Positive Affirmations** – Repeating affirmations such as "I am capable," "I am worthy," and "I am resilient" can help rewire the brain towards more positive thinking.

3. **Engage in Visualization** – Picture yourself achieving your goals and experiencing success. Visualization strengthens neural pathways that support positive expectations.

4. **Cultivate Gratitude** – Focusing on what you are grateful for shifts attention away from negativity and fosters a mindset of abundance.

5. **Surround Yourself with Positivity** – Engage with uplifting books, podcasts, and people who encourage growth and optimism.

6. **Mindfulness and Meditation** – Practices like meditation help train the mind to observe thoughts without attachment, reducing the power of negative patterns.

7. **Take Action** – Small, consistent actions toward positive change reinforce new beliefs and help break old patterns.

By implementing these strategies, individuals can gradually reprogram their minds, replacing limiting beliefs with empowering ones. The journey to mastering thought programming requires patience and persistence, but the rewards of greater confidence, resilience, and success are well worth the effort.

RECOGNIZING AND NEUTRALIZING TOXIC INFLUENCES

Recognizing and Neutralizing Toxic Influences

Life presents numerous challenges that test our emotional and psychological well-being. Among these challenges, toxic influences, whether external or internal, can significantly impact our mental health, decision-making, and overall happiness. To cultivate resilience and maintain a healthy mindset, it is crucial to recognize these influences and implement effective strategies to neutralize their effects. This section explores the various sources of negativity, both external and internal, and offers actionable approaches to establishing mental boundaries for emotional protection.

External Negativity: Dealing with Difficult People and Environments

Toxic external influences often come from people, environments, and social constructs that drain our energy and disrupt our peace of mind. These influences can manifest in several ways, including:

- **Negative relationships:** Friends, family members, or colleagues who constantly criticize, belittle, or manipulate.

- **Toxic workplaces:** Environments where gossip, excessive competition, or unrealistic expectations create stress and dissatisfaction.
- **Cultural and societal pressures:** Unrealistic beauty standards, success benchmarks, and materialistic pursuits promoted by media and social networks.
- **General negativity:** Pervasive pessimism from news, social media, or negative people we encounter daily.

Strategies for Managing External Negativity

1. **Identifying Toxicity:** The first step to managing external negativity is recognizing its presence. Reflect on interactions and environments that leave you feeling drained, anxious, or demotivated.

2. **Limiting Exposure:** Reduce time spent with toxic individuals and limit engagement with negative media. Prioritize spaces and relationships that nurture positivity.

3. **Assertive Communication:** Learn to set firm but respectful boundaries. Use "I" statements to express your needs and avoid being drawn into unnecessary conflict.

4. **Seeking Supportive Communities:** Surround yourself with people who uplift and inspire you. Engage in groups or communities that promote positivity, growth, and shared values.

5. **Practicing Emotional Detachment:** Instead of reacting to negativity, learn to observe it without internalizing it. Meditation and mindfulness techniques can help cultivate this skill.

Internal Negativity: Self-Doubt, Fear, and Limiting Beliefs

While external negativity can be detrimental, internal negativity often poses an even greater challenge. Self-doubt, fear, and limiting beliefs can erode confidence and hinder personal growth. These internal struggles may arise due to past failures, societal conditioning, or deeply ingrained self-perceptions.

Understanding Internal Negativity

- **Self-Doubt:** A lack of confidence in one's abilities and decisions, often fueled by past mistakes or fear of judgment.
- **Fear:** Anxiety about the unknown, failure, or rejection that prevents risk-taking and personal growth.
- **Limiting Beliefs:** Negative assumptions about oneself, such as "I'm not good enough" or "I will never succeed," which create self-imposed barriers.

Strategies to Overcome Internal Negativity

1. **Challenging Negative Thoughts:** Identify unhelpful thoughts and reframe them with more positive, realistic perspectives.

2. **Building Self-Compassion:** Treat yourself with kindness and understanding rather than harsh self-criticism.

3. **Developing a Growth Mindset:** View challenges as opportunities for learning rather than as failures.

4. **Practicing Gratitude:** Focus on what you have achieved and appreciate your strengths to counteract negative self-perceptions.

5. **Seeking Professional Help:** Therapy, coaching, or mentorship can provide guidance and strategies to reframe negative thought patterns.

How to Establish Mental Boundaries to Protect Emotional Health

Mental boundaries are essential for maintaining emotional balance and preventing negativity from overwhelming our well-being. Boundaries help define what we accept in our lives and what we refuse to tolerate.

Steps to Establishing Strong Mental Boundaries

1. **Define Your Limits:** Identify what behaviors and interactions make you uncomfortable or stressed.

2. **Communicate Clearly:** Express your boundaries to others with confidence and clarity.

3. **Say No Without Guilt:** Recognize that declining commitments or interactions that drain you is necessary for self-care.

4. **Protect Your Energy:** Engage in activities that replenish your mental and emotional reserves, such as meditation, exercise, or creative pursuits.

5. **Prioritize Self-Care:** Regular self-care practices reinforce boundaries and ensure that your emotional needs are met.

By recognizing and neutralizing toxic influences, both external and internal, individuals can cultivate a healthier, more fulfilling life. Through intentional efforts, it is possible to create an environment conducive to personal growth, peace, and resilience.

The Science of Resilience and Emotional Regulation

The Importance of Emotional Flexibility

Emotional flexibility is the ability to adapt to different emotional experiences and adjust reactions accordingly. It allows individuals to navigate life's ups and downs with resilience rather than being overwhelmed by adversity.

Why Emotional Flexibility Matters

- **Enhances Problem-Solving:** Adaptable individuals approach challenges with a solution-focused mindset.
- **Promotes Well-Being:** Emotionally flexible people experience lower stress and better mental health.
- **Strengthens Relationships:** The ability to regulate emotions helps in maintaining healthy interpersonal relationships.

Techniques for Reducing Stress and Anxiety Through Cognitive Reframing

Cognitive reframing is a psychological strategy that involves changing negative thought patterns to more positive and constructive ones.

Steps to Cognitive Reframing

1. **Identify Negative Thoughts:** Recognize automatic thoughts that contribute to stress and anxiety.
2. **Examine the Evidence:** Challenge the validity of negative assumptions.
3. **Replace with Balanced Thinking:** Develop a more realistic and positive perspective.
4. **Practice Regularly:** Consistency in reframing thoughts strengthens mental resilience.

Examples:

- Instead of "I'll never be good at this," reframe it as "I am still learning and improving."
- Instead of "Everything is going wrong," reframe it as "I am facing challenges, but I can find solutions."

Developing Self-Awareness to Control Emotional Impulses

Self-awareness is key to emotional regulation, allowing individuals to recognize their emotional triggers and manage responses effectively.

Strategies to Enhance Self-Awareness

1. **Journaling:** Writing about emotions and experiences helps identify patterns and triggers.

2. **Mindfulness Practices:** Meditation and deep breathing enhance present-moment awareness.

3. **Seeking Feedback:** Constructive feedback from others provides insight into behavioral tendencies.

4. **Reflection:** Taking time to analyze emotional reactions leads to better self-understanding.

By strengthening emotional regulation and resilience, individuals can navigate life's challenges with confidence and maintain a stable, positive mindset.

CHAPTER 14

THE SPARK WITHIN UNDERSTANDING THE ROOTS OF MOTIVATION AND MENTAL TOUGHNESS

Introduction: Lighting the Inner Fire

Before every great leap, every quiet comeback, and every impossible win, there's a flicker—an inner spark. You've felt it before. It's that fire in your chest before you try something bold. That stubborn voice saying "keep going" when everything in you wants to quit. This chapter is about that spark: **where it comes from, what fuels it, and how to keep it burning,** even when the world throws water at your flame.

Motivation and mental toughness are two sides of the same coin. One gives you the "why," and the other gives you the "how." But both are wildly misunderstood. People throw these words around like confetti, "Just stay motivated!" "Be mentally tough!" as if it's that easy. Spoiler alert: it's not. But it is **possible**, and it all starts by understanding the roots.

Let's break it down.

1: What Motivation Really Is (And Isn't)

We often think motivation is this magical lightning bolt that strikes out of nowhere. One day you're lying on the couch, the next you're climbing mountains. In reality? Motivation isn't magic. It's a system, and it's not always loud or flashy.

Intrinsic vs. Extrinsic Motivation

- **Intrinsic motivation** is the internal drive. It's when you do something because it aligns with your values, lights you up, or brings you joy. It's painting because it relaxes you, running because it clears your mind, or learning a new skill because it makes you feel alive.

- **Extrinsic motivation**, on the other hand, is fueled by outside forces, money, praise, social approval, deadlines. It's working overtime for a bonus or hitting the gym to impress someone else.

Both matters. But when we rely too much on the external stuff, we burn out. The most sustainable, soul-fueling motivation? That comes from within.

Debunking Hustle Myths

Let's get real about the "hustle culture." The idea that you have to grind 24/7 to be worthy is toxic. Motivation isn't about never resting; it's about knowing when to push and when to pause. True drive doesn't shout, "go harder." It whispers, "go smarter."

Myth: If you're not always motivated, you don't want it bad enough.

Truth: No one is motivated all the time. Discipline bridges the gap when motivation dips.

Mental Toughness Decoded

If motivation is the spark, mental toughness is the shield. It's what keeps you moving when things get messy, because, spoiler alert, they always do.

Toughness ≠ Toxic Stoicism

Mental toughness gets confused with being emotionless. But being tough doesn't mean never crying or pretending you're fine when you're not. Real toughness is **feeling everything and still moving forward**.

- **Toughness** is staying steady under pressure.
- **Resilience** is bouncing back when you fall.
- **Toxic stoicism** is denying emotions to appear "strong."

True mental toughness honors emotion. It just doesn't let emotion drive the bus.

How It Works Psychologically

The brain thrives on patterns. Mental toughness builds when we train ourselves to respond rather than react. It involves:

- **Emotional regulation:** Feeling the feelings but not being ruled by them.
- **Cognitive reframing:** Turning "I failed" into "I learned."
- **Self-efficacy:** The belief that you can figure things out, even if you don't have all the answers now.

Just like muscles, mental strength grows with resistance.

Why We Quit (And Why We Don't)

Quitting isn't always about weakness. Often, it's about exhaustion, fear, or overwhelm. Understanding these psychological roadblocks can help you see your own patterns.

Burnout: The Silent Motivation Killer

Burnout isn't just stress; it's stress with no relief in sight. It creeps in when we push too hard for too long without a break or sense of reward. Signs include:

- Emotional numbness
- Constant fatigue
- Loss of joy in things you once loved

Fear: The Master of Disguise

Fear often wears different masks:

- **Perfectionism**: "If I can't do it perfectly, I won't do it at all."
- **Procrastination**: "I'll start tomorrow… again."
- **Comparison**: "Why try if someone else is already doing it better?"

The trick isn't to eliminate fear; it's to move forward with it in your backpack.

The Psychology of Grit

Researcher Angela Duckworth defines grit as **passion + perseverance**. Gritty people aren't always the smartest or most talented, they're just willing to **stay in the game longer**. They have "stickiness." And stickiness beats brilliance over time.

Your "Why" – The Anchor of Resilience

Let's talk about the heartbeat of it all: your **why**.

Your "why" is the deeper purpose behind your goals. It's what gets you out of bed when the motivation is gone, what keeps you grounded when life spins sideways. Without it, goals become empty checkboxes.

Finding Your Why

Ask yourself:

- What matters most to me right now?
- What would I still care about if no one else was watching?
- What kind of person do I want to be through this process?

Your "why" doesn't have to be grand. It just has to be **honest**.

Purpose Fuels Consistency

When your purpose is aligned, showing up becomes less about willpower and more about identity. You don't need to "get motivated to work out" if you see yourself as someone who values health. It's just what you do.

Think of your "why" as the North Star. You may get off course, but it always brings you back.

Real Talk – Micro-Case Studies of Everyday Grit

You don't need to be a Navy SEAL or Olympic athlete to embody motivation and toughness. Real strength often hides in plain sight, in classrooms, kitchens, and corner offices.

Case Study 1: Maya, 43 – Single Mom, Night School Warrior

Maya works two jobs and goes to night school to finish her nursing degree. She failed her first anatomy exam and almost dropped out. Instead, she found a study buddy and carved out time between shifts to review flashcards. Three semesters later, she passed with honors.

Her motivation? "I want my son to see that we don't quit when it's hard. We pivot; we push."

Case Study 2: Kevin, 29 – Former Addict Turned Marathoner

Kevin used to drink to numb the pain of childhood trauma. He hit rock bottom after losing his job and a close friend. Through a support group, he started running, at first just a block. Now he runs half-marathons and helps mentor others in recovery.

His secret? "Running taught me that every step forward counts, even when it's ugly."

Case Study 3: Ana, 35 – Burned-Out Executive Who Chose Peace

Ana was the picture of success, six figures, high-rise apartment, constant stress migraines. She realized she wasn't living; she was surviving. She walked away, took a year off, and built a coaching business rooted in balance and intention.

Her wisdom? "Motivation is not always about going faster. Sometimes, it's about choosing a different path altogether."

Pulling It All Together: The Real Spark

So what lights the fire? It's not a one-time lightning strike. It's built from the inside out, from clarity, from small wins, from rest, from showing up even when you don't feel like it.

Here's what to remember:

1. **Motivation comes and goes, discipline and purpose stick around.**
2. **Mental toughness isn't being invincible; It's being real and resilient.**
3. **Fear is part of the deal, walk with it, not away from it.**
4. **Burnout doesn't mean you're weak; it means you need a reset.**
5. **Ordinary people do extraordinary things when they stay rooted in their why.**

This chapter isn't about turning you into a productivity machine. It's about helping you **trust your inner spark**, even when it flickers. Especially when it flickers.

Because that spark? It's still there. Even in the dark. And now, you know how to keep it .

GRIT IN ACTION DAILY HABITS, ROUTINES, AND MENTAL TOOLS THAT BUILD STRENGTH

Grit isn't something you're born with. It's not some elusive superpower granted to a lucky few. Grit is grown, nurtured through choices, shaped by mindset, and fueled by daily action. This chapter is about the "how." Less inspiration, more perspiration. Less hype, more habit. Let's talk about what grit actually looks like in real life, and how you can build it, one day, one decision, one routine at a time.

Discipline Over Hype: Why Routines Beat Inspiration Every Time

Inspiration is a spark. Discipline is the firewood.

We love a good motivational video or a TED Talk that makes us want to leap into action. But let's be honest, motivation is unreliable. It fades. It's mood based. Discipline, on the other hand, is your dependable friend. It's not always exciting, but it shows up even when you don't feel like it.

Why routines matter:

- **Consistency beats intensity.** Doing a little bit every day is more powerful than burning out in a burst of effort.

- **Routines reduce decision fatigue.** When your actions are automatic, you conserve willpower.
- **They create momentum.** A solid morning or evening routine sets the tone for your entire day or wind-down.

Real-life example:

Kobe Bryant was known for his 4 a.m. workouts. Not because he felt like it, but because he had trained himself to show up whether he was "feeling it" or not. That's grit. That's routine in action.

Your move:

Build a simple, repeatable routine that supports your goals. Start with a basic framework:

- Morning: Wake up → Hydrate → Move → Mindset reset (journal, meditate, visualize).
- Workday: Focus block → Break → Stretch → Refocus.
- Evening: Reflect → Unplug → Prepare → Rest.

Don't aim for perfection, aim for repetition.

Habit-Stacking for Motivation: Tiny Changes That Compound Into Massive Wins

You don't need a total life overhaul. You need a strategy that sneaks change into your existing rhythm. That's where **habit-stacking** comes in.

Coined by James Clear in *Atomic Habits*, habit-stacking is the art of linking a new habit to something you already do. It makes the behavior automatic, frictionless, and almost invisible.

Formula:

"After I [current habit], I will [new habit]."

Examples:

- After I brush my teeth → I will say 3 affirmations.
- After I start the coffee maker → I will write down my top 3 priorities.
- After I check my email → I will do 5 deep breaths.

Why it works:

- You're piggybacking on existing neural pathways.
- It reduces resistance and planning fatigue.
- Over time, these micro-habits snowball into real transformation.

Want grit? Stack habits that reinforce your identity as someone who doesn't give up.

Mini-habit stack for mental toughness:

- After I feel stressed → I will say, "I've done harder things."
- After I fail → I will write one lesson I learned.
- After I succeed → I will note how I showed up with grit.

Grit Tip: Don't wait for motivation. Stack habits that *generate* motivation.

The Power of Self-Talk and Mental Rehearsal: Inner Voice Training, Visualization, and Reframing Setbacks

Your brain believes what you tell it, especially when you repeat it.

Mental grit starts with the inner voice. The words you say to yourself in the quiet moments shape how you show up when it matters most. Self-talk isn't just "rah-rah" positivity. It's a psychological tool used by elite performers, therapists, and Navy SEALs alike.

1. Inner Voice Training

Your self-talk falls into two categories:

- Supportive ("I can figure this out.")
- Sabotaging ("I always screw this up.")

To shift it:

- Catch the thought.
- Challenge it (Is it true? Helpful? Productive?)
- Change it (What's a better phrase?)

Example:

Instead of "I'm so behind," say, "I can only start from where I am. Let's go."

Key phrase to adopt: "This is hard, but not impossible."

2. Visualization and Mental Rehearsal

Olympic athletes don't just train their bodies, they train their minds by mentally rehearsing every detail. Why? Because the brain can't distinguish between a vividly imagined action and a real one. You can wire yourself for resilience and success before you even start.

How to visualize:

- Find a quiet moment.
- Close your eyes and picture yourself navigating the hard moment, calm, confident, capable.
- Replay it like a movie. See it. Feel it. Succeed in it.

Use this before:

- Presentations
- Tough conversations
- Big goals

3. Reframing Setbacks

Resilient people don't see failure as a final stop, they see it as feedback. They *reframe* it.

Instead of:

- "I blew it." → "I'm learning what doesn't work."
- "This is the worst." → "This is data. What can I do next?"

Grit builds when you refuse to let hard moments define you.

Bend, Don't Break: How to Recover Quickly from Mental Dips and Emotional Challenges

Resilience isn't about never falling; it's about getting back up faster. Everyone hits walls. Everyone questions themselves. The difference? Gritty people don't stay down long. They've got recovery tools.

Here's your mental toughness first-aid kit:

1. Name It to Tame It

When emotions run high, clarity runs low. Naming your feelings can lower their intensity.

- "I feel anxious." → Ok. Why?
- "I feel overwhelmed." → What's the top stressor?

Labeling gives you control back.

2. Create an "Anchor Routine"

What do you do when you feel like you're spinning out?

An anchor routine is a go-to sequence that helps you reset.

Example:

→ Go for a 10-minute walk

→ Journal 3 lines: "Here's what I know. Here's what I can do."

→ Text someone positive.

→ Drink water and breathe.

Not glamorous. Just grounding.

3. The 5x5 Rule

Ask: "Will this matter in 5 weeks? 5 years?"

This perspective shift can stop the spiral of overreaction.

4. Micro-Breaks to Avoid Burnout

Burnout doesn't come from working hard. It comes from never *pausing*.

Grit needs breaks to recharge:

- 5-minute stretch
- Nature walk
- Music blast dance break
- Doodling or daydreaming

Recharge isn't a reward. It's a requirement.

Tools of Titans: Resilience Practices from High-Performers

Grit isn't a personality trait. It's a toolkit, sharpened by practice and pattern. Let's peek into the toolboxes of those who thrive under pressure.

1. Athletes: Serena Williams, Michael Phelps, Simone Biles

- **Routine as ritual.**
- Phelps visualizes every stroke before entering the pool. Simone Biles anchors herself with calming rituals.
- **Failure as fuel.**
- Serena's legendary focus comes from learning through loss. She doesn't avoid failure—she mines it.
- **Mantras matter.**
- "I can. I will. End of story."

2. Entrepreneurs: Sara Blakely, Elon Musk, Oprah Winfrey

- **Sara Blakely's failure game:**
- Her father would ask, "What did you fail at this week?" If she had nothing to say, he was disappointed. She learned early that failure meant *you were trying*.
- **Oprah's journal practice:**
- Grounded in gratitude and vision. She turns pain into purpose.
- **Elon Musk's mental model:**
- First-principles thinking, breaking challenges down to basics, rather than following assumptions.

3. Creatives: Maya Angelou, Stephen King, Beyoncé

- **Stephen King's writing discipline:**

- Two thousand words *every single day*. No matter what.
- **Beyoncé's alter ego ("Sasha Fierce"):**
- She used this persona to channel boldness on stage until she could embody it naturally. Mental grit, performance style.
- **Maya Angelou's clarity:**
- "You may not control all the events that happen to you, but you can decide not to be reduced by them."

Your takeaway:

You don't need to be a genius or a millionaire to build grit. You just need to study how they recover, how they reframe, and how they *repeat* the small stuff relentlessly.

Final Thoughts: Becoming the Person Who Keeps Going

Grit is grown. Not overnight. Not with hype. But with the quiet, often boring decisions you make daily:

- To show up.
- To keep going.
- To bounce back.
- To believe in yourself when it feels absurd to do so.

You don't need to feel like it. You just need to start.

Let this chapter be your call to arms. You've got habits to stack, routines to commit to, a voice to train, and a future self to grow into.

So, the next time life throws you a curveball? Smile. You've trained for this.

CHAPTER 16

THE LONG GAME: STAYING RESILIENT THROUGH LIFE'S CURVEBALLS

Imagine standing on a sprawling beach just as a storm brew on the horizon. The first gusts of wind tug at your clothes, whispering of the tempest to come. You can see the churning waves that lie ahead, each one promising to crash with a force you might not be prepared for. Life often mirrors this scene, a series of curveballs that catch us off guard, challenging our ability to remain steady amidst uncertainty. Whether it's the sting of failure, the monotony of routine, or the daunting unknown, these moments test our resilience in ways we never anticipated.

Yet, within the heart of each challenge lies an opportunity to redefine what it means to persevere. Holding fast doesn't mean fighting every wave; rather, it means learning to ride them with grace and intention. In this chapter, we'll uncover how sustaining motivation and toughness long-term is not simply about enduring life's storms but embracing them. Through stories and strategies, I'll guide you to discover ways to maintain resilience without losing sight of your goals, even when faced with uncertainty, failure, or boredom.

Resilience is a Lifestyle

Imagine a ship sailing through uncharted waters. While the voyage might sound exhilarating, it also comes with its fair share of unexpected storms and treacherous paths. Much like this ship, our lives are full of uncertainties and challenges. The key to steering through them lies in understanding and embracing the power of a long-term purpose. When you have a clear destination in mind, you can navigate through any unpredictable territory with greater ease, knowing precisely why you embarked on the journey.

Having a long-term purpose serves as a compass. It allows you to focus on what truly matters, enabling you to dismiss distractions that don't align with your goals. When life throws its curveballs, and everything seems chaotic, a well-defined purpose gives you a reason to stand strong and push forward. It is what motivates you to get up each day, even when you're not immediately gratified. Purpose isn't just about the end goal; it's about the journey and the growth you experience along the way.

Consider Sarah, who set her sights on creating a community garden in her neighborhood. She envisioned a space where people could connect with nature and each other, build relationships, and foster a sense of belonging. The path wasn't easy. Sarah faced resistance from local authorities, skepticism from the neighborhood, and financial constraints. Yet, her passion for the project kept her going. On days when progress stalled and frustration reigned, her long-term vision of a thriving community garden kept her resolute.

Purpose also acts as an emotional anchor. It provides something stable and reliable to hold onto when emotions run high. Life's unpredictability often tests our emotional reserves. During such testing times, a clear sense of purpose aids in emotional regulation, reminding us of the broader picture and why enduring short-term discomfort might lead to long-term fulfillment. The garden was Sarah's anchor. Through each hurdle, she reminded herself of her dream and what it could offer others.

However, while a long-term purpose serves as the roadmap, adaptability is the flexibility needed to traverse unforeseen paths. Think of adaptability as the ship's ability to adjust its sails to the changing winds. In our quest to achieve our goals, situations will arise that demand change, shifts, and transformation. Adaptability allows us to respond with agility, making sure we remain on course even if the route changes.

Take Tom, for example. He aimed to climb the corporate ladder in his marketing career. Yet, midway, he recognized the industry was rapidly moving toward digital. Instead of resisting or feeling defeated about his existing skill set becoming obsolete, Tom embraced the change. He adapted, undergoing training to equip himself with digital marketing skills, ensuring he stayed relevant and valuable to his organization. By combining his long-term purpose of achieving professional success with adaptability, Tom transformed a potential setback into an opportunity.

For many, adaptability is not innate. It requires practicing mindfulness and an openness to learning. It challenges you to remain curious, defy comfort zones, and be willing to embrace new experiences. As we adapt, we foster resilience, making us more equipped to handle the curveballs life has in store. When Sarah was met with bureaucratic delays and financial hurdles in her gardening project, it was her ability to pivot strategies that ensured the project continued to evolve.

Combining a long-term purpose with adaptability creates a powerful mechanism for overcoming life's challenges. They feed into each other, with each enhancing the other's effectiveness. A purpose-driven life encourages adaptability by setting a clear target to strive for. In turn, adaptability ensures that even if obstacles appear, the dream remains alive, evolving with time and circumstance. Both traits bolster mental and emotional resilience. They allow you to remain hopeful, persistent, and strong in the face of adversity.

However, what do you do when progress seems to stall or when you fall into repetitive life patterns, feeling as though you're treading water? These scenarios can drain motivation and make you forget why you began in the first place. First, it's vital to acknowledge these patterns without judgment. Understand that feeling stuck or facing routine monotony is a part of the journey rather than a failure of it.

One practical strategy is to reevaluate your goals. Are they still aligned with your purpose? Do they require modification in light of new circumstances or changes in your interests? Taking time to reflect allows you to redefine or fine-tune your direction, rejuvenating your motivation. This recalibration can often reignite the passion you felt when you first set out on your path.

Meanwhile, seeking out new challenges or experiences, even within a stagnant routine, fosters creativity and progress. When feeling trapped, sometimes a small change, exploring a different hobby, attending a workshop, or meeting new people, can provide a fresh perspective and inspiration. Adaptability again plays a role, encouraging you to willingly seek change rather than fear it.

Additionally, cultivating patience is crucial. Resilience doesn't equate to an absence of struggle; it means enduring and growing through it. Recognizing that progress isn't always linear can be comforting. Celebrate small wins, and remember: every step, even backward ones, contributes to the overarching journey.

Recognizing stalled progress or repetitive cycles is the first step. Embracing these moments as periods for introspection and growth can convert frustrations into opportunities. As you move forward, equipped with a long-term purpose and adaptability, they're navigable, empowering you to continue your journey with resilience.

In our next section, we delve deeper into practical strategies and mental shifts needed to handle these plateaus effectively. We explore how to transform the dull into dynamic and lead an invigorated life, no matter how routine it seems.

Mastering the Plateau

In the daily grind, routines often become so monotonous that you might feel as though you're idling in neutral, stuck in a rut where progress feels neither here nor there. When progress stalls, it can be tempting to throw your hands up and walk away. But there are ways to reignite that spark and renew your drive even when motivation seems elusive. Take, for instance, the experience of Sarah, an elementary school teacher who reached a point where her passion for teaching seemed to have disappeared. Each day felt the same as the last, and she wondered if she should leave the profession altogether. But instead, Sarah focused on making small adjustments to her daily activities, helping her rediscover the joy and intrigue she once had.

The first strategy is to set micro-goals. Large goals can be daunting, and the path to achieving them often involves prolonged periods of seemingly small, mundane steps. Break down these major goals into smaller, more manageable mini goals. Look at Jake, who is working toward a promotion at his job. The gap between where he is now and where he wants to be felt vast, leading to discouragement and stalled effort. By setting micro-goals, like learning a new skill each week or networking with one new person monthly, Jake created a sense of progress and momentum. Each micro-accomplishment served as a reminder of his capability and the progress he was making, motivating him to continue pushing toward his larger goal.

Another effective practice is intentional reflection. When life feels stagnant, take a moment to review where you've been and what you've achieved so far. Pause and write down three things you've accomplished in the past year that you're proud of. This exercise helps regain perspective and reassures you of your capability to grow and achieve. Imagine Lena's scenario: she spent months perfecting her business idea, but years on, the monotony of managing daily operations began to wear down her enthusiasm. Through regular reflection, Lena was able to identify the aspects of her work she found fulfilling, such as creating new products and working directly with customers, rejuvenating her excitement for the day-to-day.

Exploration becomes essential to combat repetitive life cycles. Introduce a sense of novelty by learning something new or revisiting an interest that's fallen by the wayside. Todd, for instance, enrolled in a cooking class, something he used to enjoy in college but had stopped pursuing when adult responsibilities took over. This provided him an outlet for creativity and helped break the monotony of his everyday routine, ultimately impacting his outlook on all aspects of life positively.

Mindful detachment from the idea of constant progression supports resilience during stalled periods. It's crucial to accept that plateaus are natural and necessary parts of any journey. A key aspect of this mindset involves recognizing and celebrating non-linear progress. Marcy was training for her first marathon and was disheartened when she didn't see improvements in her time for weeks. Through conversations with other runners, she came to understand that plateaus can be a time when the body is adjusting and strengthening, even if the results aren't immediately visible.

This acceptance allowed her to appreciate the invisible progress and remain patient and persistent.

Cross-training your skills is another method to enhance resilience during stagnation. Switching focus temporarily to develop complementary skills can reawaken interest and engagement in your primary pursuit. For example, an architect might benefit from taking a course in digital art to enhance their design techniques, thereby gaining fresh ideas and perspectives to apply when returning to their traditional work.

Purposeful acts of kindness can transform mundane days into moments of genuine connection. Helping someone else not only helps them but also gives you a different perspective. For instance, volunteering at a local shelter helped James, an analyst inundated with numbers and deadlines, find meaning beyond work, providing a fresh sense of fulfillment and revitalizing his spirit upon returning to his personal and professional obligations.

Incorporating these resilience-building practices into daily life seamlessly connects the larger purpose of achieving long-term goals with the necessary adaptability to handle life's smaller ebbs and flows. These strategies prepare you not only to handle current repetition but also lay the groundwork for tackling more significant challenges.

But what about bigger setbacks—like failure or grief? Understanding how to maintain equilibrium during these can fortify your overall resilience. Picture Lucy, who experienced both professional rejection and a personal loss within months. By having already practiced maintaining resilience through the smaller stagnations in life, she found herself better equipped mentally and emotionally. Lucy's journey through these tougher times conveys that handling life's repetitive patterns equips you with skills and strategies that translate broadly, enabling you to withstand and eventually overcome even the most formidable disruptions.

While the road is never completely straight or smooth, those daily measures, the micro-goals, reflections, new explorations, and moments of connection, pave the way to sustain the momentum even amidst the ambiguities and plateaus. Think of them as the rhythmic beats of an ever-evolving dance, guiding you smoothly and surely, step by step, toward your future goals, carrying you past today's hurdles into the arena where larger life obstacles can be faced with courage and resilience.

Motivation in Crisis

The journey through life's curveballs often begins long before the actual impact. Previous insights focused on recognizing the signs of stalled progress and acknowledging repetitive patterns. Whether it was taking a moment of reflection to see where things went off track or reaching out for support to break the cycle, these strategies lay the foundation for building resilience. As you move deeper into understanding resilience, these earlier tools transform from mere survival tactics to integral parts of maintaining strength in the face of significant disruptions.

Imagine standing in front of a giant wave, representing grief, failure, or another setback. The fundamental techniques you already practice are like the surfboard that keeps you afloat and directed. But now, we add layers, paddle skills, balance adjustments, to ride those waves of life more skillfully and with determination. Developing internal strength is crucial for not only enduring immediate challenges but enhancing the quality of life. It's about rewiring thought patterns, reshaping emotional responses, and seeking strength within vulnerability.

Think about this: resilience isn't just a tool for when you face personal downturns; it's adaptive. It spills over into relationships, impacts your work, and influences health. Strengthening your resilience now sets you up for future successes across your life. As you explore these principles, remember this section serves as the bridge. It's your transition point from managing moments of stagnation to diving into resilience that changes everything, your interactions, your career, and your wellness.

To plant seeds of resilience, try integrating mindfulness. The next time an emotional tsunami threatens to overwhelm, pause, and focus on the present moment. Imagine Jane, who lost a job she loved. Contentment turned to despair as uncertainty loomed large. Instead of dwelling on what had been, Jane chose mindfulness. She spent time every morning aware of her breath, in tune with her surroundings, even if all she focused on was the hum of traffic or the rustle of leaves. This practice grounded her, creating a calm space amid chaos.

To get started with mindfulness, follow these steps:

- Find Your Space: Choose a quiet spot free of distractions. Whether it's a corner in your bedroom or a nearby park bench, select a place that feels safe and uninterrupted.

- Breathe With Intention: Close your eyes gently. Inhale deeply through your nose, hold it for a few seconds, and then exhale slowly through your mouth. Focus only on the rhythm of your breath.

- Acknowledge Thoughts, Then Release: As thoughts trickle in, simply acknowledge them. It's natural for your mind to wander. Picture them as clouds drifting by—note them, then let them float away without attachment.

- Develop Consistent Practice: Commit to a set amount of time, even five minutes initially, and gradually increase it as your comfort grows.

Mindfulness becomes an anchor, steadying as external situations ebb and flow. The clarity it provides echoes in responses to pressure, whether in personal dialogues or demanding work meetings, extending beyond personal obstacles into our interaction with the world.

Consider journaling as another method. It offers a safe expanse to unravel emotions and trace the threads of thought. Picture Mark, experiencing grief after losing someone dear. Through journaling, he found a conduit for feelings he couldn't articulate aloud. By writing down his frustrations and moments of yearning, Mark illuminated pathways toward acceptance and healing. The lineage of a journal entry provides insights into the psyche, weaving understanding into everyday experience.

Steps for effective journaling include:

Create a Routine: Dedicate a specific time each day to writing. Your journal becomes a constant companion. Morning or night, consistency transforms it into a healthy habit.

- Let Words Flow Freely: Don't censor or edit. Your journal is for you alone. Let the words tumble out, imperfect and raw, capturing the true essence of your thoughts and emotions.

- Reflect With Purpose: Occasionally revisit past entries, reflecting on emotional growth or recurring themes. This hindsight positions you for better understanding and control over future responses.

- Embrace Different Mediums: Whether you express through words or sketch out images, exploring different styles can free creative energies and expose deeper inner truths.

Both mindfulness and journaling are portals not just to endurance through hardships but also keys to personal transformation. They channel inner dialogues into constructive comprehension and lend clarity to muddled emotions.

In times of uncertainty, failure, or boredom, consider these frameworks the core disciplines of resilience. They are your companions on this long journey with life's ups and downs. From this middle ground of building mental and emotional strength, future sections will delve into resilience's broader implications. How do these skills enhance relationships? How does resilience empower professional environments or health pursuits?

In fostering this resilience, you've established a cycle of growth. Your internal support systems, from breathing exercises periodically anchoring you to journaling sessions elucidating emotional layers, become reliable allies. They bring stability to turbulent times and reinforce not just the ability to endure but to flourish with intention and confidence. The aim here is not simply to cope but to fuel a life rich with vigor and purposeful living. Resilience transforms challenges from hindrances into catalysts for overall life enhancement, making this section not just beneficial but essential.

Mental Toughness Across Life Domains

In the face of life's challenges, resilience becomes the vital undercurrent that guides us through choppy waters. Previously, you've explored the art of staying centered during grief and setbacks. Now, let's expand on this foundation and navigate relationships, work, and health, crafting resilience in each sphere.

In relationships, maintaining resilience begins with empathy and open communication. Picture a couple facing the tension of everyday trials; their schedules always seem out of sync, conversations often misfire over long workdays, and the seemingly small frustrations start piling up. The practice of resilience here isn't about avoiding conflict or pretending everything is fine. Instead, it's about choosing to approach each other with patience and understanding, even when emotions run high. For instance, setting aside dedicated time to discuss feelings and concerns can reshape their dynamic. They don't just talk about surface-level issues but delve into the root causes of their triggers, using "When you say this, I feel..." statements to foster understanding rather than defensiveness. Over time, this commitment to compassionate dialogue fortifies the relationship, enabling it to withstand external pressures.

At work, resilience often requires balancing ambition with adaptability. Consider someone who just received feedback they weren't expecting on a significant project. The initial sting can feel like failure, but resilience invites a reframe. Instead of dwelling on the critique as a personal deficiency, they see it as an opportunity for growth. This perspective shift transforms the critique into a steppingstone, a chance to hone skills and improve. To strengthen this resilience, they might set up a feedback loop, regularly seeking insights from peers and mentors to fine-tune their approach and ward off stagnation. The notion of adaptability emerges here as well; being open to altering methods or perspectives when something isn't working. By embracing this flexibility and understanding feedback as a positive catalyst, they cultivate a resilient mindset that can navigate through the labyrinth of unexpected twists in their career journey.

In terms of health, resilience is about forging a partnership with one's body and well-being. Imagine someone juggling a demanding job, family responsibilities, and their desire to stay fit. Exercise might seem like another box to check, but resilience reframes it as an act of self-care that sustains both the body and the mind. When their energy wanes, resilience suggests gentle adaptability instead of rigid persistence. Perhaps on particularly exhausting days, swapping a high-intensity session for a calming walk revitalizes them. Emphasizing rest, resilience affirms the necessity of listening to what the body communicates. Another example is how someone dealing with a chronic condition might thrive by building a support network that includes doctors, advisors, and perhaps a community of others facing similar challenges. This community becomes a wellspring of encouragement and shared wisdom, reaffirming the notion that resilience often flourishes in connection, even in the realm of personal health.

To experience these resilience skills firsthand, engage in this exercise tailored to personal relationships. It's called "The Connection Ritual," and it emphasizes fostering a deeper bond through resilience:

Connection Ritual Steps

- Identify Shared Challenges: Together with your partner, identify a shared challenge or recurring tension in your relationship. Keep the focus on shared issues to avoid single-sided blame or negativity.

- Set the Stage: Choose a calm, uninterrupted environment for the ritual; this could be a cozy corner of your home or a peaceful park spot. Make sure both of you have the time and emotional space to engage fully.

- Active Listening Exercise: Agree to take turns speaking and actively listening. Set a timer for 5 minutes. During this time, the speaker describes their experiences and emotions surrounding the challenge, while the listener practices active listening, maintaining eye contact, nodding, and demonstrating empathy without interruption.

- Reflect Together: Once you both have spoken, reflect together on what you've heard. Use statements like, "I understand that you felt..." or "I didn't realize that my actions made you feel...".

- Brainstorm Solutions: Collaboratively brainstorm solutions. Focus on flexibility and adaptability. How can you both address this challenge creatively? What small changes can you implement that support your bond?

- Commit and Check-In: Choose one shared action you can take within the week to address the challenge. Schedule a follow-up check-in to discuss progress and feelings toward the new approach.

- Practicing these rituals nurture resilience within relationships through communication and adaptability. It offers you a structure to face tensions together, grounded in empathy and understanding.

Look beyond basic applications and consider how these resilience techniques can be adapted as life evolves. Each area demands unique strengths, whether deriving from clearer communication, embracing feedback with grace, or balancing personal needs with life's demands. But they're all tied by a common thread: the conscious choice to meet adversity with the capacity for growth and transformation.

Next, consider how this resilient mindset paves the way for a broader focus on long-term impacts. Resilience transcends beyond immediate survival, gradually shifting towards crafting a life that fuels lasting fulfillment.

Legacy Thinking

In our exploration of resilience, we've seen how it weaves through our relationships, propels us in our work, and stabilizes our health. These areas serve as the groundwork for a mindset aimed at creating lasting impact. This leads us naturally to legacy thinking. As we navigate life's unpredictability, we often lose sight of the broader picture, caught up in immediate tasks and challenges. Legacy thinking shifts this focus. It invites you to consider a broader vision, emphasizing how each decision and action contributes to the mark you leave behind.

Imagine an artist obsessing over each brushstroke but missing the beauty of the entire painting. Life can feel like that too. You spend days consumed by trivial matters, but legacy thinking teaches you to step back. It pushes you to envision your life as a whole, composed of countless small actions that build something enduring and meaningful. This perspective doesn't just add significance to your actions, it also fortifies your resilience. The moment you view your efforts as contributions to a greater purpose, mundane tasks become part of a compelling narrative.

Lee, a teacher who dedicated over thirty years to a small-town school, exemplifies this mindset. At first glance, her routine might seem repetitive: grading papers, attending meetings, and overseeing the same school events. Her legacy, however, isn't merely in those tasks. It's in the students she inspired and the futures she helped shape. Lee's vision was never about checking boxes; it was about fostering curiosity and passion for learning. By focusing on the long-term impact of her work, she found renewed energy and motivation even on the most challenging days.

In practical terms, cultivating this mindset requires a blend of introspection and action. Start by identifying what you value most. What principles guide you? Your answers become pillars for your legacy, offering clarity and direction amidst life's chaos. Consider Maria, who discovered her passion for environmental conservation later in life. Although her job didn't involve this field, she started volunteering in weekends, planting trees, and organizing community clean-ups. Her professional life might not have changed dramatically, but her legacy did. Her actions reflected her values, creating ripples of impact in her community.

Long-term goals act as anchors, keeping you steady and focused. They prevent you from swaying with daily distractions. By having these clear objectives, you develop resilience to withstand temporary setbacks. Take Sam, an aspiring author who faced rejection after rejection. He kept writing, continuously refining his craft because he valued the stories he wanted to tell. His legacy wasn't about the immediate success of a bestseller list, but the books he aspired to leave for future generations. Understanding this kept his passion alive and shielded him from discouragement.

Legacy thinking also encourages you to embrace adaptability as a tool for resilience. By viewing challenges as opportunities to learn and grow, you align with the idea of life as a journey rather than a destination. You might encounter a detour in your career, a personal health issue, or a relationship setback. Each curveball becomes less daunting with a legacy-oriented mindset. Instead of fixating on the detours, you adjust and continue to move forward, enriched by the experience.

Embracing a vision for long-term impact also means recognizing your interconnectedness with others. No legacy is born in isolation. It involves a tapestry of shared experiences and collective growth. Being part of something larger encourages you to seek collaboration and support from those around you. In doing so, you find strength in the community, drawing on shared resilience to overcome difficulties.

Think of Nia, a community organizer whose legacy thrives on her ability to unite people. Her projects may face challenges, but her focus remains on the bonds she strengthens and the positive changes she ignites within her community. This connection with others not only amplifies her impact, but it also provides the resilience she needs to keep moving forward.

You cannot overlook the importance of gratitude in cultivating legacy thinking. Appreciation for those who contribute to your journey fuels a positive outlook, reinforcing your resolve during tough times. Expressing gratitude acknowledges the interconnected nature of life, encouraging you to celebrate both small and significant accomplishments along the way.

To build this legacy-oriented resilience, practice regularly reflecting on your journey. Set aside time to evaluate your progress towards long-term goals, celebrate wins, and reassess strategies. This habit keeps your vision sharp, motivation high, and actions purposeful.

Resilience is not just about surviving life's curveballs. It's about thriving through them by maintaining a vision that reaches beyond the immediate horizon. Legacy thinking lifts you above the daily grind, giving those grindstones the weight of meaningful purpose. It challenges you to view each action through the lens of its contribution to your legacy.

So, as you step out into the world each day, remember that your journey is not just about the tasks at hand. It's about embedding each step, each choice, with a sense of greater purpose, creating a roadmap for lasting impact. By doing this, you cultivate a resilience that not only withstands the rigors of life but transforms them into steppingstones for a legacy worth leaving behind.

Final Insights

Nicci Brochard & Dr.Ben Chuba

As we've journeyed through the concepts of sustaining motivation and resilience, it's evident that these traits are not merely about overcoming difficulties but embracing them as part of life's tapestry. Now that we understand how a long-term purpose coupled with adaptability strengthens our emotional and mental fortitude, we can chart a path that navigates uncertainty, failure, and even boredom with unwavering resolve. By setting clear goals and practicing flexibility, we align our daily actions with broader aspirations, transforming challenges into opportunities for growth. This approach not only reinvigorates our motivation but also enriches our life's narrative, guiding us towards enduring fulfillment and achievement. As we look ahead, let this newfound resilience empower us to face future hurdles, knowing that each step forward builds the legacy we aspire to create.

EPILOGUE

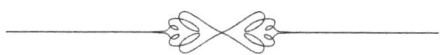

The Power is Yours

As you turn the final page of this book, remember that you have the power to shape your thoughts, emotions, and experiences. The techniques and insights shared here are not mere theories; they are practical, powerful tools ready to be used in your daily life.

Negativity will always exist in some form, but you now understand that you are not at its mercy. You have the ability to challenge harmful thoughts, replace them with constructive ones, and resist the pull of doubt and fear. Every time you practice mindfulness, reframe a situation, or choose gratitude over complaint, you strengthen the foundation of a positive and resilient mindset.

Focus is another key that unlocks your potential. In a world filled with distractions, your ability to direct your attention toward what truly matters will determine the quality of your life. Whether through meditation, structured routines, or simply a conscious effort to be present, maintaining focus will keep you moving toward your goals with clarity and purpose.

And happiness? It's not found in grand achievements or distant dreams; it exists in the small, everyday moments. The laughter of a loved one, the warmth of the sun on your face, and the simple pleasure of a deep breath are the treasures of life. By training yourself to notice and appreciate them, you cultivate a state of joy that is independent of external circumstances.

Your journey doesn't end here; it is only the beginning. Keep practicing. Keep growing. Keep choosing positivity. Every thought you nurture, every emotion you manage, every moment you fully embrace brings you closer to the life you deserve, a life of clarity, peace, and fulfillment.

The power is, and always has been, yours. Now go and use it.

ACKNOWLEDGEMENT

B en and I would like to express our deepest gratitude to you who contributed to the creation of **Managing Your Subconscious Mind and Emotions:** *Techniques to Resist Negativity, Stay Focused and Positive, and Find Happiness in Daily Activities*. You know who you are. You are dear to us. This book project would never have come full circle without the unwavering support and encouragement of our family and friends. You inspired us to explore and research the exciting potential of the human mind and subconscious.

A special thank you to the crew at Cross Border Publishers and colleagues, whose wisdom and insights have shaped the ideas within these pages. The reviews and feedback were invaluable. To our readers, we are profoundly grateful that you considered reading this book. Your openness to embark on this journey of self-discovery and personal growth is amazing. We feel blessed and encouraged to be part of that transition.

Finally, we extend our appreciation to the countless reviewers, editors, and experts whose hard work illuminated the path toward emotional resilience and mental clarity. May this book serve as a guiding light in your pursuit of happiness and inner strength. We hope that you have gotten what you were looking for. Please, kindly leave us a review.

Thank you.

Nicci

www.ingramcontent.com/pod-product-compliance
Lightning Source LLC
Chambersburg PA
CBHW071521120626
46550CB00006B/2306